HOW TO WHOLESALE HOUSES FOR HUGE CASH

HOW TO WHOLESALE HOUSES FOR HUGE CASH – PART II

(With Contracts Included)

&

REAL ESTATE MARKETING. HOW TO BE A REAL ESTATE MILLIONAIRE

By Ernie Braveboy

Get Your Free Copy of

How to be a Real Estate Millionaire

To Get Your Free Copy, Open the Link

https://ebraveboy_3ee2.gr8.com/

Respective authors own all copyrights not held by the publisher.

The information herein is offered for informational purposes solely and is universal as so. The presentation of the information is without a contract or any type of guarantee assurance.

The trademarks that are used are without any consent, and the publication of the trademark is without permission or backing by the trademark owner. All trademarks and brands within this book are for clarifying purposes only and are the owned by the owners themselves, not affiliated with this document.

TABLE OF CONTENTS

How To Wholesale Houses for Huge Cash

ERNIE BRAVEBOY

INTRODUCTION

I want to thank you and congratulate you for buying the book, "*How To Wholesale Houses for Huge Profits*".

This book has lots of actionable information that you can use to wholesale houses for huge profits.

Wholesaling is one of the fastest growing fields in the real estate market today. It appeals to people much in the same way options trading in the stock market does: it comes with vastly minimized risk and does not require you to spend a lot of personal time or money.

The thing is; a good wholesaler who is ready to do what it takes to be good in the field will be great in no time. The good thing is that real estate wholesaling is not a complex field at all; everything about it is simple and organized.

This book will show you how to be an effective wholesaler who can close multiple deals in short periods. It will also show you the fun side of wholesaling, and point out why you should consider taking wholesaling seriously. Let's begin.

Thanks again for buying this book. I hope you enjoy it!

ERNIE BRAVEBOY

Before we can get to a place of discussing how to wholesale houses for profits, it is important to build a strong understanding of what wholesaling entails first. Therefore, if you are a beginner to the field of real estate wholesaling, it is important that you start from the very beginning so that by the time we get to the point of discussing real estate wholesaling, you understand the concept fully. Let's begin.

THE BASICS OF HOUSE WHOLESALING: WHAT EXACTLY IS IT?

Wholesaling is a term house flippers and real estate investors use when talking about the process of joining the dots between buyers and sellers and picking up a check for their efforts. Think of a finder's fee—you may not own the item or asset, but you made it possible for the person who needs it to get it and you make money for making this happen.

When you conduct your wholesaling business in a legal manner, something many investors fail to do and pay dearly for, you can make a lot of money. However, to generate these amounts of money, you have to be smart about wholesaling, and be willing to buckle down and work hard.

With this in mind, what exactly is wholesaling? What does it comprise of?

Rather than go on a winded, technical explanation on what wholesaling is, here is an example to help you fully understand what wholesaling is.

A Wholesaler's Tale: Meet James the Wholesaler

James is a wholesaler. He spends his days looking for the best real estate deals he can find. However, he is not interested in truly getting in to these deals. One day while he is at his favorite coffee shop, he gets a call from Nora, his friend since high school. She wants to sell her house but is not interested in the usual motions of using an agent. She mentions to James that the house could use a few repairs but that she only wants to get rid of it since she does not want to direct any more money into fixing it up.

James decides to have a look at the house. He looks at the condition of the house and notes the repairs that need doing. He offers Nora a price of $75,000 for the house. Nora accepts on the spot. They both sign a purchase agreement. This agreement points that James or any other party he assigns this contract to may buy the property within the next 15 days for a price of $75,000.

James knows of a friend who mentioned in passing that he is an expert in flipping houses and completes several deals every month. Let us call him Joe. James calls Joe and tells him of the house. He makes sure to mention the necessary repairs needed and how much it could be worth after repairs (known as A.R.V or **After Repair Value**). James offers to sell the property to Joe for $80,000.

Joe knows that after fixing the house up, he can make a good profit. He agrees to the price. James and Joe sign an 'assignment contract', which legally means that James is allowing Joe to purchase the property from Nora. James can do this since he signed a purchase agreement with Nora saying that either James or another party could buy the home in 14 days.

How does all this play out? After everything goes through, Joe will pay Nora $75,000 and James will keep the extra $5,000 as a finder's fee. In the real estate industry, this finder's fee is what we call a wholesale fee.

Can you see how potent this is?

James never truly owned the house yet he made $5,000 off it because he acted as the link to Nora and Joe. Such is one of the ways a wholesaler will structure deals and make profits.

You now have an understanding, albeit a general one, of real estate wholesaling. But I know you might be thinking; is this even legal? That's what you will learn next.

THE REAL DEAL WITH WHOLESALING: IS IT ILLEGAL?

You may have noticed that James, the wholesaler, signing both a purchase agreement and an assignment contract with the respective characters in the story.

As far as the legality of real estate wholesaling goes, there is usually a lot of debate surrounding it. Is it legal to wholesale? Some people will say wholesaling is okay, and they are right. Others will say it is not, and will not be wrong either. In truth, there is no black and white answer since the laws on wholesaling differ from state to state.

Staying Within Legal Boundaries

However, as is the cases in every other field, use of sheer common sense can help us determine some illegalities. If, for example, the paperwork is shady, the wholesaling is illegal.

The other thing is that even though laws differ from one state to the next, some hard and fast rules apply everywhere. For instance:

1. It is illegal for anyone who is not a realtor or broker to sell a home for a third party. This is why, if you go back to section 1, an assignment contract had to be in place before Joe, the 3rd party in the story, could become truly involved.

2. It is illegal for a wholesaler to receive a commission. The only people who are privy to a commission are realtors or brokers. If you have it in your contract that you are to

receive a commission for a sale, you are operating outside your legal boundaries and can be subject to prosecution. This brings us to the next part of this chapter.

A Comparison between Legal and Illegal Wholesaling

Here, we shall look at the characteristics of both:

Illegal Flipping and Its Salient Characteristics:

1. Its main intent is usually to defraud somebody, usually the buyer.

2. The buyer is usually unsophisticated and earns a low income.

3. The property sells at a low price and at retail price, or higher.

4. The seller will be unclear on issues surrounding repairs and will do only that which is necessary to cover up defects.

5. There may be collusion with an appraiser to get a price that is higher than retail price.

On the other hand, legal wholesaling is usually open and between two people who are relatively sophisticated. As you may have guessed, honesty is critical and there is strict adherence to legal channels before any transactions happen.

A Legal Wholesale Transaction Will Look Like This:

1. The buyer and the wholesaler will enter a transaction openly with the intention of making a profit

2. There is no fooling or taking advantage of the buyer. There is a level of sophistication as far as he or she is concerned.

3. If the buyer buys the property at a truly low price, its selling price will be considerably below retail price.

4. The wholesaler may choose not to do any repairs to the property. The buyer will determine exactly what needs doing and will estimate both the cost and the A.R.V

5. The buyer will complete his or her own appraisal based on several factors, among them personal experience.

6. There is no lender. As such, there is no bank fraud.

The next question you might have is; what's in it for you? What's so good about wholesaling, which makes it a great income opportunity? That's what you will discover next.

WHAT'S IN IT FOR YOU?

What puts off most new investors from getting started on house wholesaling?

For the most part, the fear of failing when dealing with investments that require large inputs of cash or lots of time before maturity is what puts off many people from getting started. Lack of sufficient money, knowledge, and skill, in this case as regards real estate and rehabilitation, plays a big part as well.

If you are new to house flipping, wholesaling is the best place to start. It does not need a lot of startup capital. If anything, apart from asking you to invest your effort, work super hard, and understand real estate law with regard to wholesaling, it does not ask for much else. There is a lot less risk in wholesaling compared to, say, buying a property outright.

Why You Should Wholesale

Here are reasons why you should consider wholesaling

1: You Do Not Need a Lot of Money to Get Started

To get started as a real estate wholesaler, you do not need a large bank account. Putting a house under a purchase contract and then assigning the contract does not require much money. If you are dealing with motivated sellers, the amount of money you need could be as little as $1.

2: You Do Not Have to Take Ownership of the House

When assigning the contracts, you do not take ownership of the property. You are not the party closing the deal and as such, are not in the chain of title at any one time. This eliminates two things: a large part of costs, and most of the risks involved with property that is most likely vacant and requires repairs to make it livable.

3: It Helps You Steadily Learn What Good Deals Truly Are

There is a wholesaling rule that holds up in just about every situation: *if you consistently have trouble selling your wholesale deals, it could be that you are asking too much or lack enough buyers.* A lot of the time, it is the former. With time, you will gain the ability to discern what makes a good deal and what does not.

4: Networking & Building Relationships All Improve the More You Get Into Wholesaling

You will occasionally sell deals to other more experienced investors. Inevitably, you will build relationships with them. If the kinds of deals you sell them are the homerun kind, they will want to be your friend. The benefits of having friendships with such successful investors are many. You could even end up with a mentor who spends years training you on how to be a better house flipper and how to determine A.R.V better.

5: It Is Easy to Wholesale Part-Time and Hold down A Full Time Job at the Same Time

You can wholesale part-time: wholesaling is not too labor intensive. Sure enough, you have to work hard to be familiar with the field, especially while starting out. However, after this, you will spend most of your time marketing and making offers. With time, your screening skills will grow to the point where you do not have to see as many houses because you instantly know which ones will make good deals and which ones will not.

With that understanding, let's now move on to the next bit i.e. wholesaling like pro by avoiding some potential pitfalls.

Well, just because the benefits above look enticing doesn't mean you should go all in on wholesaling without taking into consideration the possible pitfalls. So what is it you need to be aware of if you are to make it big with wholesaling?

A SMART WAY TO WHOLESALE: RED FLAGS TO AVOID

We could also have titled this section *"Amateur moves and marketing mistakes too many wholesalers make and that you should avoid as a wholesaler."* It is also a continuation from the previous section.

The trouble with most aspiring wholesalers is that they are impatient. They do not treat the industry with the due respect it deserves or bother to understand the laws. Thus, they flout many of these laws as soon as they start marketing themselves. Equally bad is their disinterest in creating a professional first impression and in so doing, attracting serious buyers.

Here are amateur wholesaling moves you must avoid at all costs especially when making your presence known to others as a house flipper. The reason why most people who attempt wholesaling either come away with nothing, or walk away with a bunch of lawsuits at some point or other, is that they do not put in the necessary work it takes to become as professional and informed as possible.

Amateur Mistake 1: Aimlessly Spamming Social Media Looking for Homes to Wholesale

There are too many social media posts floating in the internet made by people looking for houses to flip. Businesspeople are encouraged to use social media as much as they can. Yet, there is a smart way to go about this.

The bulk of wholesalers who advertise their businesses on social media fail to follow a clear marketing structure that allows them to appear as seriously wholesalers. Take Facebook for example; rather than having pages set up that exclusively cover wholesaling deals, many people will use their personal Facebook accounts that they use to speak on all manner of things—from poodles, to eBay purchases.

This lacks organization, is unprofessional, and defeats any intention you may have of treating your wholesaling as a business. Section 7 gives you general guidelines on how to harness social media and use it to market your business.

Amateur Mistake 2: Putting In Commission Clauses in Your Contract

Section 2 clearly states that it is illegal for anyone who is not a realtor or broker to receive commission on property sold. Too many people do not understand this one, or make sure the commission clause is the first thing on the contract. It is important to understand this: the fee you receive as a wholesaler is a **wholesaler's fee**. You are not privy to a "commission," and including this in your contract is misguided.

While it is true that you do not always have to be caught, it will be a nightmare for you if you someone sues you or takes you to court on an issue surrounding the property deal, and there is mention of this.

Amateur Mistake 3: Having No Purchase Contract and Assignment Contract in Place

This is necessary paperwork. Without this, your wholesaling activity is little more than illegal house flipping, which can get you into serious trouble. Make sure you have these signed by you and the relevant parties.

The above chapter is not meant to scare you but to prepare you for the work ahead to ensure you don't make costly mistakes while wholesaling. To prepare you even the more, the next part will discuss how much work is required if you are to excel as a wholesaler.

EXACTLY HOW HARD DO YOU HAVE TO WORK IN WHOLESALING?

Surely, wholesaling is easy, right, is that not what everybody says about it?

Here is the truth about wholesaling though: **it is hard.** If you are looking for an easy payday, wholesaling is not the field for this.

It is necessary for you to be competent in many things: to be diligent and brave. At any one moment, there will always be an investor with the capacity to outbid you and offer deals far superior to yours. The competition is often fierce and truth be told, there are just too many wholesalers around today to assume it is an easy field.

As a wholesaler, you will often have to work extremely hard to find any deals at all let alone find good deals. You will have to hustle and then hustle some more to stay relevant. A lazy and unmotivated person will usually get nowhere with wholesaling or will break laws that will lead to fines or even jail time.

In short, wholesaling is a business and as is so often the case, any business that succeeds takes a lot of hard work.

How Do Wholesalers Make Good Money?

Successful wholesalers make good money because of this simple reason: they complete multiple deals every passing month. At a standard price of $5,000 for every deal, (this is the average price in as far as wholesale fees go), you do not need too many deals. However, you have to work constantly to know more and more buyers and investors, and what they may be looking for.

To be a good wholesaler who will be around long after most have dropped by the sides, you will need a degree of skill in the following:

1. Understanding the math underlying a good flip and a good rental

2. Keeping your calm in distressed situations and maintaining a civil conversation all through

3. Negotiating with others without taking advantage of them

4. Marketing for those leads that will cost less than the marketing will

5. Cold calling as well as answering phone calls

6. Sales

7. Looking for and finding good deals

8. Estimating ARV (After Repair Value)

9. Estimating the costs of rehabilitation

10. Estimating potential rental fees

What Does All This Mean?

With wholesaling, you will have to put in consistent work. While it is possible to outsource some things, you will still need to be in charge and understand how all of these things work.

To be a wholesaler, you will have to be a hard worker who is not only good at many things, but who also knows how to socialize, reach out to people and respond to them regardless of how bad the emotional climate may be.

Up to this point in life, you may have worn the introvert label with pride. A few things will have to change. There is nothing wrong with being introverted but you will never make any progress by doing the equivalent of sitting by yourself in a full room waiting for others to reach out. You will have to be aggressive.

This section does not serve the purpose of making you rethink your decision to be a wholesaler. Its purpose is to dispel the myth that wholesaling is easy and if anything, it should fill you with hope that you will succeed. How so? Because you now know that most people who get into wholesaling will never succeed since they lack the necessary work ethic. You have a chance to be part of the few who will succeed.

With what we have learnt so far, we will now move on to discussing specific components that determine whether you excel as a wholesaler or not with the first part centering around defining your target area.

DEFINING YOUR TARGET AREA: WHERE DO YOU WANT TO WORK?

As a novice wholesaler, you cannot just assume that you will go wherever possible to find deals. It will be necessary to establish your target area; the area you will focus the bulk of your efforts to finding deals. Many investors who fail to establish a target area often find themselves spending more time than is necessary to lock down good deals. It is also true that this is the most prevalent mistake among most new wholesalers.

You need to focus primarily on one area: your target area. This will help you save time and energy you would otherwise spend scouting a new area and learning about it.

The Target Area

Ideally, your target area should be within a 10-mile radius of where you currently live. Why should you start with where you live? For starters, you probably know the area well. You are familiar with just about everything, down to the side streets. You know the good areas and the bad ones. By starting with your area of residence, you drastically shorten the learning curve. The quicker you learn, the faster you can start making money.

Get a zip code map (visit http://www.usnaviguide.com/) and find 5 zip codes around your residence. Print your map out and draw a circle that fits in the zip codes you choose. This will be your target area. Because it is in your backyard, it is likely that you know everything about it. The next step is to drive the streets and get to know the area even more than you do.

Get to know the names of the streets and the different tracts. Get to know the bad areas as well as what makes them so, and do the same with the good areas. Next, drive to work, the bank or the grocery store, look around and evaluate the area.

Look at old and ugly homes that may be ripe for flipping; take a different route home too. You can also intentionally get lost and work your way back to your place, all in a bid to get to know the area better.

Understand the kinds of houses on each block. Do you have bungalows on one block, stucco structures on another, and wood buildings on yet another block? Is the landscape rock, gravel, grass, desert, or one of large trees? Do you have mostly duplexes or triplexes? Seek to know as much as possible.

Once you've identified your target area, the next part is to find great deals.

FINDING GREAT DEALS AS A WHOLESALER: WHERE DO YOU LOOK?

They say that a wholesaler who lacks a good deal is like a butcher who has no meat: his business is useless, as is any knowledge he may have. To avoid being a meat-less butcher, you must become proficient and increasingly effective in creating a pipeline of good real estate deals.

Why use the term pipeline? Well, your goal as a wholesaler is not to do just one deal at a time. Your goal will be to do multiple deals. However, deals need careful handling, with a degree of patience, until they come to fruition. This could take some time. Thus, the successful wholesaler is consistently filling his or her pipeline with leads and working them through this pipeline.

Here is what to do to get great deals:

1: Look into the MLS

MLS is a collection of all deals currently sold by real estate agents. The competition is severe and as such, it may be difficult to get good deals. Understand that it may be hard to wholesale a home foreclosed by a bank but it is not altogether impossible.

2: Drive for Dollars

What you do here is get into your car and drive around looking for a potential deal. Your goal is to look for property you may consider "depressed." You can spot such property by viewing long grass, windows boarded up, and tarps on the roof, among other things.

3: Network Online

Social media will give you the capacity to reach many people in just one click. You should consider setting up a simple WordPress wholesale site and market yourself from it. It is a smart thing to keep buyers on various destinations too. Once you have your site up and running, link it to Facebook, Instagram, Twitter and even LinkedIn.

4: Learn About Mail Marketing & Be Good At It

You ought to buy real discount bargains well below the market value. It is necessary for a sufficient spread to be present for the end buyer to make some profit. In the event that the price tag, as far as your end goes, is too high, a property you may be unable to dispose of may mess you up.

One of the effective approaches to get decreased costs is via direct mail marketing. While it is true that direct mail marketing can be expensive, it is only so in the event that the property you intend to wholesale is in truly decrepit condition or you are too lazy to mail more than a few people. You could even blend your direct mail marketing efforts with email marketing where you collect email addresses of visitors to your website to make it easier to reach out to them when there is need. Money is in the list; if you are careful with how you collect emails and engage your list appropriately, you can be sure that your marketing campaigns will yield great leads.

5: Attend Real Estate Meetings

These days, every state has a local real estate speculation club. It does not matter what your experience level is: make sure to join your local club. These clubs are usually phenomenal places to discover great discount bargains.

As a beginner wholesaler, wholesaling is not just a way to make some money; it is also a way to gain contacts and learn more about the business. This will all begin with finding deals to buckle down and work on. By using these 5 techniques, you will find good deals in just about every market.

What next after finding great deals? What steps should you take to identify ideal properties? That's what we will discuss next.

THE IDEAL PROPERTY: UTILIZING THE BOARD OF REALTORS & THE DEPOSIT AMOUNT TO GIVE THE HOMEOWNER

What is the ideal property?

If you are advertising properly (the next section mentions how you can go about it effectively), your phone will be constantly ringing. What is the ideal property? Well, the ideal property is that which has a sufficient equity.

Consider this example of a property worth $100,000:

Understanding that the property is worth $100,000, you use your negotiation skills and scale the buying price down to $55,000. You fill out the purchase contract with the homeowner as the seller and you as the buyer.

Assume you already know a good house flipper who likes to make a certain amount of profit on every deal, and you know that you can have him purchase the property in the next week. As a good wholesaler, you will factor in his standard profit amount, as well as other costs such as miscellaneous costs (holding fees and so on) and rehab costs. Adding all these amounts together and subtracting them from the initial $100,000 figure will give you your expected profit amount. (Section 10 will go into depth on this.)

The question here is what are the easiest routes to find such property with sufficient equity?

The Board of Realtors

The Board of Realtors is a good place to start. The contracts on there are wonderfully simple, easy to read and understand, and prepared in such a way that the most unsophisticated homeowner can understand them. As such, it will be very hard for someone to adjudge you to having broken laws and taken advantage of a homeowner.

Call your Board of Realtors and ask if they sell contracts to public folk. Most states will have a Board of realtors that has no issues making contracts available to the public.

The Sales Contract

The first line will be reserved for the buyer's name. This is where you put your name. Below, will be a space for "and/assigns"- fill in the necessary information here. This will allow you to assign your contract to the prospective buyer, such as another house flipper.

The Deposit Amount

To make the contract binding, it will be necessary to leave a deposit with the present homeowner. You do not have to hurt your wallet: wholesalers occasionally leave deposit amounts as low as $1. A $25 deposit is usually sufficient. This way, if wholesaling the property becomes difficult, you will not be too much out of pocket.

Surely, a $25 deposit is too low to be taken up?

Actually, it is not. Simply put it like this, *"We usually give a $25 deposit and then make sure we close in X number of* *days (say, 50 days)."* This powerful statement is one that will always meet sellers' expectations. The only reason homeowners will reject your proposed deposit amount is because you present it all wrong. Express yourself with confidence. Once you can do this, and especially attach a specific timeframe that works for you, it is very easy to sell yourself to homeowners.

Next, we will discuss the process of wholesaling in 8 simple steps.

WHOLESALING IN 8 EASY STEPS: THE GENERAL FORMAT TO FOLLOW WHEN WHOLESALING

A successful wholesaling process typically takes 8 steps, in the order below. By following the steps below, you will successfully wrap up deals and make a profit, and do so entirely within the law.

Step 1: Marketing

This is the most vital bit in your wholesaling business. You get your business going by marketing. You need to market your business to get deals. Your marketing plan, to be truly effective, will need to comprise of a combination of social media, broadcasting, and networking.

Step 2: Make Calls & Respond to Mail

Once you start getting responses because of your marketing efforts, you need to start capturing and analyzing all the responses. After capturing the responses, the next bit is to qualify them. You will do this by tracking the mode with which you received the responses with the examples of bandit signs, e-mail, direct mail, social media, and telephone.

Step 3: Inspect Your Property

You need to understand the condition of the property and as such, its value. You will need to evaluate its renovation, if it requires it. You will get there by picking up as much information on the property as you can. You need to conduct a thorough inspection to get this information.

Understand that as a wholesaler, you do not have to give exact figures. Your job is to get the absolute best estimate, in the ballpark, and in so doing, ensure your numbers make sense. This is only possible if you fully understand the state of your property.

Step: Negotiating the Deal

Perhaps you are familiar with the saying *"You do not find a good deal, you make one."* It will be very rare for you to get a call from somebody who is willing to sell the property at 70% of the A.R.V, minus the cost of repairs. Just about every seller will want to get top dollar for the home. It will be up to you to get the best possible price and in so doing, create a win-win situation for both seller and yourself. You will have to develop your negotiation skills. As they become better, your deals will get better as well.

Step 5: Get it all Under Contract

Once you have agreed to a deal with the seller, you will need to have him or her sign a contract. It will be advisable that you learn a lot about the legal implications of transactions as well as the legal paperwork. It will be necessary for you to educate yourself on entity structuring as well as buying and sales contracts. On top of this, you need to know what to do with these contracts once you have them signed.

Step 6: Identify a Buyer

Once you have the deal under control (that is under contract), and you know you have a great deal, the next step is to advertise your deal. You can make calls to the renovators you meet in your networking groups, post the deal online using such outlets as craigslist; the list goes on and on.

Step 7: Conduct an Assignment of Contract

Once you have come to an agreement with the buyer, you will need to transfer your responsibilities and rights in the contract to the buyer. You will do this via an assignment of contact (you will have the buyer sign an assignment contract.)

Step 8: Closing Your Deal & Cashing the Check

The deal-closing bit also goes by settlement. When closing, you will sign the appropriate documents and then cash your check.

Here is a tip for you: always ask your sellers for a testimonial. A collection of testimonials will go a long way in marketing your business.

Next, let's discuss about how much to offer.

THE OFFER: HOW MUCH SHOULD YOU OFFER?

The one thing you should understand about wholesaling is that you will only make money when others are making money. Thus, you have to come up with the right offer. The amount cannot be too high or too low as this will hurt you financially in one way or the other.

Just how much should you offer?

Going by the paragraph above and understanding that you will only make money when somebody else makes money too, you will have to reverse engineer the entire dynamic. If you are selling to another house flipper, he or she will have to make a profit; otherwise, he or she will not be willing to buy the property from you. The key is to understand what they want. Even better, understand what their margins are.

Constructing Your Offer Based On ARV

Everything begins with the ARV (After Repair Value). The key is to have this number in mind. Once you do, start working backwards:

1. How much does the person you are selling to, if he or she is a flipper, aim to make on the deal?

2. What are the rehab costs?

3. What are the miscellaneous costs, such as holding costs and others?

4. How much profit do you want to make?

Now that you know the ARV figure, you will understand the highest amount you can pay on the deal.

It will look a bit like this:

Your Offering Price = A.R.V − The Total of the (Bulleted) Areas Above

Look at this example:

Jack is a wholesaler. He finds a property and because he has some experience checking out distressed property and determining its value, he determines that the value is $190,000. He knows a good flipper; he also knows that the flipper usually makes a $30,000 profit on most flips. Jack does more research, walks through the property, and checks the condition of every facility. He determines that the miscellaneous costs (commissions, closing costs, and the like) will come to just under $25,000.

Jack calls up a contractor and walks him through the property. The contractor determines that the rehab costs will come to about $40,000. Jack also knows that he wants a wholesale fee of $5,000.

This is how John determines his offering price:

Offering Price = $190,000 - $30,000 - $25,000 - $40,000 - $5,000

The price he comes up with = $89,000 (or a bit less than this)

How exactly do you keep abreast with all these numbers?

To begin with, none of this is as hard as it may appear. If you can perform basic math and have access to a generous amount of paper, it is easy to figure most of this out. It helps if you love mathematics. However, if you do not like math and are uninterested in spending thousands of dollars on a personal coach, consider a wholesale calculator. Bigpockets has a spectacular wholesale calculator you can find on:

A wholesaling calculator, such as the BiggerPockets.com one, lets you quickly determine your Maximum Allowable Offer for every potential wholesale deal. Most of these calculators are easy to use and they walk you through relevant questions in a systematic format.

We've been talking a lot about ARV but haven't really discussed how to determine the ARV. The next part will discuss just that.

MATTERS REGARDING ARV: DETERMINING ARV

The previous section mentioned the use of wholesale calculators to help you determine a proper offering price. However, the offering price will be heavily dependent on the ARV. No wholesale calculator will determine the ARV for you, and the ARV is the most vital number in the entire process of finding a good offer especially given that you will subtract every single figure from this particular one. Therefore, you must ensure you have an accurate ARV value.

How Do You Determine The ARV?

Multiple methods exist, but they all revolve around one principle: *A house will be worth roughly what similar local houses have gone for in recent times.*

Of course, it will be important to determine just how close a property has to be to qualify as local. If a property was sold 20 miles away, it may not be close enough. Other factors should play a part in determining ARV; a sold 4-bedroom house will not be similar enough to a 2-bedroom house you want to wholesale. A home was sold in an awful condition is not similar to a well-kept home.

While it is highly unlikely to find an identical home sold recently, you need to get as close as possible to recently sold homes to determine an accurate ARV. Consider every factor you think will hold some weight. Did the recently sold home have 2 bathrooms, while yours has one? Did the other home have 500 square foot less of space compared to your own? Use all these factors to determine the ARV.

An Easy Way to Determine ARV: Using Real Estate Agents

You do not have to hire the services of one: just ask intelligent questions. A lot of them are usually glad to talk about real estate, a subject they love, and they have lots of data as far as recently sold homes go. However, consider that there are agents who will not want freely give advice they consider professional. Find a way to make it worth for such ones.

One of the ways you can do this is drop them unworkable leads that hold the potential to make them some money. This will forge strong friendships that will be beneficial for you.

Once you have the ARV, let's now focus on how to talk to the seller to make an irresistible offer.

TALKING TO THE SELLER & MAKING AN OFFER: A PROCESS

After covering the steps outlined in the previous sections, the time will be ripe to put your selling hat on and make an offer.

Talking Up the Seller and Presenting an Offer

You will need to sell yourself while "devaluing" the property at the same time. This works to make the homeowner realize that the deal you are offering is a superb deal. In addition, you are offering to make a purchase "as is, where is, and with no inspection required" (this means with no need to perform any rehab measures). This means regardless of how broken down the property is, you will not need the seller to put up any rehab or repair costs.

Sell the Homeowner the Idea That You Are Taking Risks

Make sure the seller understands that you are assuming all the risk in the deal and not only are you doing this, you intend to pay cash quickly (give them a period you will operate in). You need to put forth an offer that is hard to refuse.

Few people are interested in paying repair fees of fixing up their house before they make a sale. Most times, all they want it for the house to stop being their business anymore and to have some money in the bank to show for their sale. Convince the seller that you are indeed helping him or her out.

The "Inspection Contingency" & Using It to Get the Best Deal

Traditional purchase agreements usually have an inspection contingency built into them. This means the potential buyer, which is you in this case, may back out if you do not like the look of things post-inspection.

You backing out of the deal is a massive hassle for the homeowner. The process of finding someone else to jump through all the hoops of the purchasing process is a taxing one.

Consider this three-point scenario:

- You are empowered to back out at any time

- The house is broken down to the level that it is not immediately livable and requires rehab.

- The homeowner cannot afford these repairs

A typical home inspection process is capable of tying up a house for 2 weeks or more. What is more, most traditional deals will usually take up to 45 days to close. This will mean the seller will not see any money for 2 months. In addition to this, it may be necessary to pay for house repairs just to get an interested buyer. This is quite unappealing to the homeowner. Use all of this to press your point.

An example of approaching a buyer who refuses to budge below $110,000:

"I understand you want $110K for the house. However, I am countering at $79K. Here is why: I can pay you cash on

Wednesday next week and I will buy your house "as is, where is, with no inspection". This way, you will have no repair worries, and neither do you have to go through all the hassle of inspection. You will literally have cash on hand by Wednesday evening."

Next, we will discuss how to close deals.

CLOSING THE FIRST WHOLESALE DEAL: 3 TIPS TO MAKE IT MOVE FASTER

Here are 3 tips to help you close a deal fast:

Tip 1: It Helps To "Mind Your Due Diligence"

What exactly does this mean? This means you do whatever it takes to become as educated on the subject of wholesaling as possible. Read as many related pamphlets and books as you could. Attend as many seminars as is possible. If there are any networking events you can attend, make sure you are among the first people to arrive. It helps a lot if you have a relationship with experienced hands in the game. Do whatever it takes to become relevant in the lives of experienced house flippers.

Do you know the biggest reason why most beginners fail to close even one deal? It is because they skipped this step and dove straight into trying to find and close deals. Before you do anything, take care of this stage. Give yourself several weeks to become truly familiar with the field. Those few weeks may be the difference between decades of mediocrity or success.

Tip 2: A Buyers List Is Important

A buyers list is not as hard to create as you may think. All you need to do is be a proactive person. Make sure you collect the contact information of everyone you meet, whether in wholesaling-based meet-ups, or otherwise. Record this information carefully. It will not hurt you to show some professional flair and give out business cards to people. Not everybody will call you; however, if you give out enough of them, someone will eventually pick up the phone and dial your number.

Tip 3: Make Sure To Target Motivated Sellers

What is the best technique to reach motivated sellers? It is not picking up the phone and cold calling; neither is it spamming their social media handles. The technique that really pulls the motivated sellers away from the rest of the lot is direct mail. While simple, there is directness to this method that appeals to serious sellers.

Which people will qualify as motivated sellers and thus, your primary targets? Look for delinquent taxpayers, absentee owners, owners of property who do not live in the county or state, and people with homes whose foreclosure date is near. Ideally, look for "distressed property," as this book so aptly pointed to in an earlier section.

Cash Buyers: How Do You Find Cash Buyers Quickly?

Your goal as wholesaler is to generate money and at the same time, dispose of property with as much speed as possible. This is necessary so you can focus on getting even more deals and building your portfolio quickly.

Knowing this, whom are you going to sell your property to?

The best kind of buyer will be the "cash buyer." You have likely heard of this term before. While it is a bit of a buzzword that too many gurus like to toss around, it is indeed a real thing.

Who Is a Cash Buyer?

A cash buyer will be a buyer who can pay cash for the property. This is all quite simple, or so it appears. Understand that this cash does not have to be their cash. A lot of the time, cash buyers will use hard money or private money to close a deal. The point of all this is this: The buyer does not have to go through the hassle of a lengthy loan process that is prone to rejection anyway. It is 100% guaranteed that when the day to wire the money comes, the sale should go through.

Usually, most of your cash buyers will be house flippers. However, there will be the occasional real estate developer as well. When it comes to cash buyers, the key thing to understand is that everybody is looking for a good deal these days. If you make a habit of offering good deals, you will not run out of cash buyers.

Your ideal buyers list, for everything mentioned in this book, will comprise of 100% cash buyers. If this is not possible, ensure most of the people in it are cash buyers. With this said, there is a lot of hype on finding cash buyers. There are many thousand-dollar programs floating around. Many of those programs are overpriced and overhyped. Save some money and follow the following advice:

Cash buyers are easy to find. However, they are only easy to find after you have done everything else right. If you do so, you will quickly discover that cash buyers are everywhere.

How do you find them though?

Craigslist is a good option. The ads you put on there are free. Paying for a newspaper ad is also an option. However, one of the greatest ways that always works is to ask a real estate agent to provide you with a list of every home within a radius of 20 miles that was a cash sale. This is easy data to get. After doing this, perform some public searching of records to know who bought those homes and then send them mail or cold call them.

After closing the deal, what next? Let's find out.

POST-DEAL ACTIVITY & GETTING PAID

If you do everything else in this book and do it well, the next logical step is to get paid. Everything else leads to this. Getting paid will mean you can further expand your wholesaling business. It will also mean a lot as far as having some extra money goes.

You have taken the time to learn as much as you can on wholesaling. You have worked to find the best deals. You have done a thorough job of assessing the property and determining the ARV. You have worked on your math and you know how much you will offer the seller to make a profit on the deal.

You have done what it takes to attract cash buyers to you and build a sizable buyers list. Everything is ok and all that is remaining is to have the money wired to your bank account. What do you need to know about this process? What can you expect and how do you move forward?

Getting paid

This may well be the easiest and most straightforward process in this entire package of process. This is because there will not be much for you to do. All you need is to get all the information to the title company. This is inclusive of every contract you have signed. After this, you sit back and wait. If you are in a state that does not use Title Companies and instead uses attorneys, you will get the information to the closing attorney; they should take care of everything else, if they are competent.

Try working with a title company or attorney familiar with wholesaling. Too many of them are unfamiliar with it. If you are unsure of the best one for you, ask some local wholesalers to help you out.

At the end, the seller will get the money promised. The cash buyer is going to get a superb deal. As for you, well, you will become a little richer.

What are you going to do with your money though? Will you buy a new car? Will you finally overhaul that dated wardrobe you own?

All this is ok but if you are a smart wholesaler, you will view this money as an investment and will make sure to channel it into your marketing budget so that you keep a full pipeline. A single deal will not transform your life. However, creating a good pipeline that consistently delivers good deals certainly will change it.

With that in mind, let's now discuss some general guidelines to keep in mind while going about your business as a wholesaler.

GENERAL ADVICE: THE KINDS OF WHOLESALERS YOU DO NOT WANT TO BE

You do not want to be any of the following wholesalers:

1: The Miss-Informed Wholesaler

This wholesaler is the kind of person who refuses to be smart while looking for deals, especially when building a buyers list. Why do new wholesalers think they can skip doing the actual work and get a $100 buyers list from "a source" that will forever transform their lives? This mistake is one often made despite being one of the more foolish mistakes.

To build a good buyers list, you have to put in the work by actively searching for cash buyers and motivated sellers. You need to build your contacts in an organic manner; this requires time and effort.

2: The "I Am Not Too Sure I Want To Be A Wholesaler" Wholesaler

This fellow gives a story like this: "Last week was absolute bliss. Seriously, it was great! I caught up with 5 of my friends and there was so much to gossip about we talked for 8 hours straight. Can you believe we even forgot all about eating during that period? We did not even have water. All this time, my phone was ringing off the hook; some cash buyers who picked the absolute worst time to call. Well, I put it on mute so that I could call them after I was done gossiping with my friends. After all, what are we without our friends?"

3: The Cheap Wholesaler

This sort of wholesaler will usually have a story that goes like this: "I sent out over 5,000 letters last month. I only got 5 calls, and none of them were from motivated sellers, if sellers at all. Their replies all went like this, "I was about to throw the piled up letters in the bin when I saw your letter. I only picked it up because I thought it was a bill. I am sorry but I am not selling my property." Well, I figure next month will be a better month for me."

You have to do more than just send letters. You need to get into your car and drive around the neighborhood looking at property. It will do you good to pick up the phone and cold call. Make sure to cultivate relationships with real estate agents, other wholesalers, and house flippers. Spread your net as wide as you can and build as many relationships as possible. The more you know, the more likely you are to close a good deal.

ERNIE BRAVEBOY

HOW TO WHOLESALE HOUSES FOR HUGE CASH

PART II

ERNIE BRAVEBOY

INTRODUCTION

I want to thank you and congratulate you for buying the book, "how to wholesale houses for huge cash (part 2 with contracts included)".

This book has a lot of actionable and authoritative information on how to wholesale houses for huge cash.

You've always wanted to dip your business feet in real estate, to strike it big in the field, and through it, fashion a better life for yourself. You know you can do it because not only do you have the requisite work ethic necessary to survive in what is often a cutthroat business, you are willing to do whatever it takes and learn whatever you need to learn to become a successful real estate investor. Nevertheless, one thing has consistently shut the real estate investment door in your face: your lack of funds.

If you can relate to this, you may be in luck; the phenomenon of wholesaling may very well be the solution to your lack of funds problem. If you're willing to work hard and smart, you can succeed in real estate without necessarily having much in the way of money.

This book will guide you through wholesaling. It'll teach you everything you need to know to not only become a great wholesaler but one who stays on the right side of the law without necessarily muffling his or her ambition and aggression in getting business done.

The content in this book seeks to build on what the first book cover. By the end of this book, you should be a much more complete wholesaler in terms of business mentality and acuity.

Thanks again for buying this book. I hope you enjoy it!

WHOLESALING 101: WHOLESALING AND REAL ESTATE IN GENERAL

Book 1 introduced you to being a wholesaler. This section and the rest of this book will build on what you learned in book one so that, by the time you turn the last page of this book, you will become a more refined wholesaler.

What better place to start than at the one constant element present in just about all things, real estate wholesaling included, *the element of change.*

Adapting To Change: Technology and Its Stronghold on People

In recent years, people have been moving away from desktop PCs to laptops, and from laptops to tablets and smartphones. This can only mean that compared to 5 years ago, today, people are getting their information from different avenues. They are also relying a lot more heavily on the internet and social media for their "information fix" than they have been at any other point in time. It's for this reason that you should:

Start with old school methods but a transition to digital platforms and with time, lean heavily on them:

When you first start out, I encourage (as most experts in this field will tell you) to begin with older methods of finding properties and self-marketing. Here, think of strategies such as driving in search of houses or putting up bandit signs to let the neighborhood know of your presence (beware that the latter will also let the authorities know of your presence.) Book 1 recommends this, for a fact.

Doing this (using old-school methods) is necessary because of it:

1. Gives you firsthand practical experience

2. Toughens your hide against rejections and failed deals

3. Makes you get better at prospecting motivated buyers and ideal properties

4. Being on the ground where you deal with people directly and take people you think will be valuable to your development for drinks and such is a good way to build your network and market yourself.

However, to really grow, you have to be increasingly less traditional and more digitally oriented because in a vastly digitized world, going digital is the best way to reach more people and find more houses to wholesale or sell.

Therefore, you should consider modern marketing avenues such as:

1. **Twitter:** Set up a Twitter account that broadcasts to everyone that you are a wholesaler. Getting re-tweets and mentions will lead to great exposure.

2. **Facebook:** Like Twitter, set up a Facebook account, complete with images and multiple relevant posts, that shows your wholesaling intent.

3. **Set up a Site:** Set up a simplistic blog or website that markets your business and perhaps display some relevant ads there. This way, you make money twofold: by wholesaling and revenue from paid ad clicks. However, don't overdo with the ads, as you could easily make your website/blog to look less professional.

By going digital, you instantly cease being just local; you become global and everyone around the world has a chance to know you and make deals with you. By moving onto social media and the internet, you expose yourself to the world and get a chance to grow your brand exponentially.

Can you see why this is powerful? To make matters even better, social media and internet use will work passively for you most of the time; however, you still need to update your footprint online and track what people are saying about your business and brand.

With a bit of basic on what it takes to be a successful wholesaler in the current times, let's now tackle something else; how to become a wholesaler even if you have no money.

CAN YOU ACTUALLY WHOLESALE WITH ZERO MONEY DOWN?

In just about every article or piece on wholesaling, you will see people marketing their service by telling you that you can begin wholesaling with absolutely no money down. No matter how you look at it, this looks too good to be true. Still, the people who tell you that you can wholesale with no money down repeat the same thing because it's not entirely untrue. Let us get to it and debunk this if it indeed deserves debunking.

Can you wholesale with no money down?

The correct answer is yes... and no.

As you saw in Book 1's story of James the wholesaler, it is indeed possible to wholesale with no money down. However, this book has to admit that the story of James glossed over and overly simplified something, the part where James gets the call from Nora, high school friendship notwithstanding. The truth is:

You have to spend so as not to spend:

This subtitle is likely to sound like a riddle- that is not intentional. Let us go back to James example. Would you say James ended up being a serious prospect to Nora because he stayed inactive and idle? The answer is no, and you cannot really chalk it up to the two were high school friends. Nora was looking to make a sale (and make money) not to catch up with an old friend. She had to do what was best for business.

At its core, wholesaling is a marketing game. It, therefore, makes sense that the best wholesalers are also the best marketers. If there ever were a hard and fast marketing rule, the rule would be that marketing is rarely free and the more effective it is, the more costly it is.

Let us examine James' situation, and just how he may have been able to not only have Nora seek him out, but have Joe as a business friend and thus, be able to finalize a wholesale deal in a matter of days.

At first, James may have had nothing to go by. His portfolio was only stacked in his imagination, he lacked any clientele, and he likely did not know Joe. To get somewhere, James may have had to be very proactive. He may have:

1. Fueled his car and scouted his immediate neighborhood looking for properties he could start with. James may have advanced his scouting so that he scoured the entire county in search of properties on sale and in an attempt to grow his client base and portfolio. Fuel costs money and driving around like that certainly takes up time. James could have easily used this time to make money from a conventional avenue such as working overtime at his day job.

2. James may have "interned" with a seasoned wholesaler where he had to pay the said wholesaler a fee to show him the ropes as well as show him how to close deals quickly and make valuable friends in the business. The wholesaling veteran may have been kind enough to introduce him to one or two contacts so that he could get started.

3. James may have spent money on books—such as the money you've spent on this book—to be able to learn all he could on wholesaling and what he needed to do to break the ground. He, of course, had to act on the knowledge he gained from the books, but purchasing the books or brochures was the first step.

4. James could very well have paid an experienced wholesaler for the service of an introduction to some clients or just their phone numbers, something many aspiring wholesalers do. Granted, it's not quite as organic as what this book teaches you, but there is nothing illegal about it and if you can, you should go this route as well.

There are dozens of scenarios that James could have put himself in to advance himself, but the constant element is that he had to spend some money to get ahead. You are now in a position to understand what the "yes...and no" answer points to. Can you wholesale with no money down? Yes, you can...but you really cannot.

Next, we will be discussing how to become a lean wholesaler.

BECOMING EXTRAORDINARY: MOLDING YOURSELF INTO A LEAN WHOLESALER

At this point, you are more than familiar with the standard definition of the wholesaler as a professional. Let's take that understanding a step further and shed more light on the unique group of real estate investors called wholesalers. Beyond the standard definition, who are they really, at least with regard to other real estate investors?

Wholesalers are real estate investors whose talent and reputation is too often overshadowed by hasty, less-experienced wholesalers who ultimately give the whole group a poor reputation.

The 2 Kinds of Wholesalers

Going by this definition, it is apparent that there are two kinds of wholesalers. The first group, the group that means business, is that of the out-and-out professionals, and the 2nd group is that of those who cannot be bothered enough to understand the intricacies of the wholesaling business, have no regard for ethics and structure, and often end up in trouble with the law.

This section of this guide shows you what you need to do to be an outstanding wholesaler with the utmost professionalism.

What Makes a Phenomenal Wholesaler?

The answer to this question is simple: to be considered a phenomenal wholesaler, you need to have ALL the traits of a real estate pro, combined. What does this mean?

1. A great wholesaler needs to be a rehab guru (one who buys subpar property, fixes it up, and sells it off).

2. He or she needs to be an expert in the ways of the landlord (one whose specialty is purchasing property to rent out).

3. He or she needs to be a real estate agent (one who looks out for and finds properties for the rehab gurus and landlords).

All of this looks too tall an order to meet especially if you take it at face value. What this means, however, is that to become complete as a wholesaler, you need to be familiar with all, and combine all the three mindsets. This section is not asking you to become a landlord, a property rehab expert, or a real estate agent even though the latter has multiple similarities to what it means to be a wholesaler. This section is simply asking you to seek to understand what each deals with, goes through, looks out for, and seeks to accomplish in multiple scenarios.

These three individuals have unique traits that allow them to succeed.

1. A rehab guru has the uncanny ability to visualize what a property will look like after fixing up, and what its value will be relative to its present, unrepaired state.

2. The landlord has the ability to view the property and determine if it will give him value for money when rented out.

3. A real estate agent is great at finding "diamonds in the rough."

What can you do to merge all three mindsets into one? Two things:

1. You need to learn as much as you can. It is important that you read as much material as you can on all three kinds of investors. If you can attend seminars, do it. If you can talk to seasoned professionals in all three real estate professions, set up appointments with them and follow up on any calls you make; few things beat listening to seasoned people talk about their professions. They often provide deep insight, which they often take for granted. They are also very happy to share since most people rarely ask for the insight—they mostly focus on money.

2. Seek to experience what they deal with as closely and as first hand as you can. Try your hand at wholesaling rentals and residential properties alike. Learn until you become or almost become who they are. In the acting circles, they call this sort of intense study an embodiment of values and, most importantly, experience, as "method," as in "method acting." Seek to become a "method wholesaler" who knows the ins and outs of all three real estate professions.

The True Skill of a Phenomenal Wholesaler

What have we been building up to and what is the ultimate skill you will be looking to develop by doing all this? Let us have a bit of a preamble before getting to this:

Real estate is risky; to transition from merely making money to being successful, you will have to take multiple risks. Some properties will not convince you wholesomely even when the potential is there to see. If you are to survive and thrive in this business, you cannot pass up on every deal that does not promise 100% profits. Thus, taking risks and venturing into the unknown will be your reality as a wholesaler.

By seeking to combine all three mindsets, you will minimize your proneness to mistakes even as you take risks. You will get infinitely better at taking educated risks. Thus, the "true" skill you will be after is that of taking an educated risk. How is this viable?

Well, with so much knowledge picked up and firsthand information on what to expect with different property types and scenarios, you will often KNOW what a property offers and what it does not. This very quality may see you thrive in the business while so many others pull out.

Now that you understand the mindset and skills you should strive to build to be a successful wholesaler, in the next chapter, our focus will be on finding deals.

FINDING DEALS: ACTIONABLE STRATEGIES YOU CAN USE TO FIND DEALS QUICKLY

This section builds on a similarly titled section/chapter in Book 1 and offers more insight on how you can acquire wholesale deals, especially if you are just starting out. It will do you good to combine the material here with what we covered in Book 1.

The best way to find deals is to know what you are looking for in the first place. This should be your starting point; everything else should progress from there. With that in mind, here are several strategies you can use to find properties:

1) Aggressively search the classified ads be they online or offline. Do not be too general in your search, as this will then mean that you have to search through a lot of chaff to get something that is ideal for you. You should streamline your search by including such terms as "needs rehab work," "owner carries," "urgent sale," "looking for quick sale," "investor special," and the like. Such terms are also handy in getting you to come across "motivated sellers," a subject covered in detail in the next section.

2) Advertise your services. Often times, the best way to do this is via social media. If you have a good Twitter or Facebook following, it helps a lot to advertise on these platforms and encourage your friends to spread the word. If you want to go a step further, consider paid ads on other people's websites and blogs (pay per click being especially viable.) The latter may cost you considerable

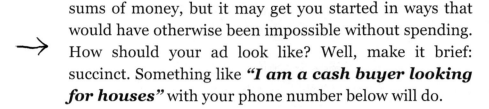

sums of money, but it may get you started in ways that would have otherwise been impossible without spending. How should your ad look like? Well, make it brief: succinct. Something like ***"I am a cash buyer looking for houses"*** with your phone number below will do.

3) Seek out seasoned real estate agents and realtors and establish a relationship with them, do them a favor of some sort so you get their attention, or intern for them for a while. Why bother with this? Because real estate agents and realtors understand real estate circles and know motivated sellers who should be your number 1 target as a wholesaler. The idea is to seek an introduction to such people or simply their contacts. It is not quite as organic as the other strategies here, but it works well and helps you begin business faster.

4) Use car magnets and bandit signs. These can display such messages as "I buy houses and pay cash." To be honest, these are not what we would call "entirely legal." However, the most you will face from the authorities are phone calls demanding that you take them down. By then, you should have made some headway. Bandit may not be the most professional or best way to find houses, but they are extremely effective at getting you through to people who are not technologically shrewd or are uninterested in searching the internet for buyers.

5) Attend your local real estate club meetings. While there's no guarantee that you will get deals directly from doing so, such meetings provide you with the opportunity to

network with wholesalers and buyers, which may ultimately help you greatly.

As you scout for deals, it is important that you understand a phenomenon referred to as a 'motivated seller' phenomenon.

THE MOTIVATED SELLER PHENOMENON: UNDERSTANDING WHAT A MOTIVATED SELLER IS AND HOW TO FIND ONE

The section above mentions that finding motivated sellers should be your number one priority. As one who is new or relatively new to wholesaling, this rings very true. However, let us begin by noting that the real estate circles vastly overuse the term "motivated seller" to a point where too many people have little or no idea of what it means anymore. So, what does "a motivated seller" mean? What makes somebody a motivated seller?

Recognizing the Motivated Seller

More often than not, the motivated seller draws motivation from two primary factors: *money* and *time*. Often, the two overlap to a point of being the same thing. If you have ever been in a situation where you needed money urgently and needed it quickly or some undesirable developments would occur, then you understand what this means.

The motivated seller is often looking to sell his or her house within a short period to both make money and wash his or her hands off the house fast. A lot of the time, the house itself is just as much of a problem as the lack of money. We could thus say that a motivated seller is one who is hard-pressed to sell a house quickly and make money off it within as short a period as possible.

How do you recognize prospective motivated sellers?

Here are several factors to keep an eye on for when determining a motivated seller. The factors here do not cover the whole range of motivated seller situations but they are by far the most common and you will rarely go wrong with them:

1) The seller's home is either in or near foreclosure. Looming foreclosure completely changes the seller's landscape when it comes to making a purchase. There is no time to let sentiment get in the way of a sale (think something like overpricing the house because the seller's personal valuation of it far outweighs what its really worth.) There is no time to fix up what needs fixing up so that the seller can get a better price for it. The only way forward is to sell off the house as fast as possible. A seller facing foreclosure will usually be very willing to sell it off at a far lower price than he or she otherwise would without the foreclosure pressure.

2) There has been a death in the family and family members are looking to offload the house quickly. Many houses in the U.S go into the market immediately after the owner passes on. This is perhaps because the family is seeking to raise funds to balance out some debt the deceased accrued or it could be that moving forward, the maintenance costs will be too steep and thus unmanageable. It could also be that the family wants to move to a new neighborhood. Whatever the reasons are,

you will often find that the sellers deliberately underprice the house to move it on quickly.

Here are several more factors:

1) There is a divorce, which compels the quick sale of the house. This is often very common since the house's value is often part of the alimony calculations.

2) The seller has made a few terrible investment decisions and he or she needs quick money to fix his or her mess.

3) The seller has built a new house and has not been able to sell off the old house yet.

4) The seller is looking to get rid of a vacation home since he or she feels there is little reason to keep owning it.

5) A job transfer that compels the seller to move to another locality and thus, he/she has to sell off the old house.

6) The seller has already moved and is impatient to sell off the old house quickly to make some money and avoid maintenance costs of a house he or she is not living in anymore.

Assuming that you find a motivated seller, you will undoubtedly need to see the house, as this is the first step to closing a deal. Let's discuss that next.

GOING TO SEE THE SELLER'S HOUSE: WHERE TO LOOK AND WHAT TO YOU LOOK AT

Visualize this. You have had the good fortune of receiving a call from a motivated buyer, and she wants to know if you can begin looking at her house so she can sell it off immediately. Like the smart wholesaler you are, you have told her to wait until you have visited her house and conducted a thorough inspection, something that should not take too long to do.

After agreeing to arrive at her house tomorrow at 8.00 am, you hang up and begin working on the necessary purchase and assignment contracts. There's one kink though, this is your very first wholesale deal. You have never visited a potential seller's house before with the intention of selling it off.

In short, you are not sure what to do. So what do you do? How can you make sure you conduct the inspection right so that you can make the right assessments, peg an appropriate price to the house, and ensure that at the end of the day, you make a profit? That's what we will be discussing in this chapter.

What You Should Do

Here are the several steps to take to ensure you do a thorough job of looking at the house:

1) Make a good first impression, which means show some manners by warmly introducing yourself to the seller.

2) Once done with the introductions, ask the seller if she minds if you take some pictures. If you are truly keen on getting off on the right foot, you need to take pictures so that you can use them to crunch the numbers at your own pace later. There will come a time when you will not need to take any pictures when you will be able to estimate property value just by looking it over, but this knack is one you will have to build with experience. For now, pictures will be necessary.

3) Take many pictures, as many as 50-100 pictures. That sounds like a lot. However, it is vital that you take that many pictures. As a new wholesaler, you may not have the knack to estimate any rehabilitation costs as well as property price in the short time you are on your seller's property. You may also not be comfortable with calculating rehab costs in front of the seller. Having lots of pictures allows you to take your time, once you are back at your place, and make the right estimates based off of the large amounts of "evidence" at your disposal. When it comes to the picture:

   a) Take several angles of the sides, exterior front, the back, roof, garage, sidewalk, driveway, and a couple of the street view each way.

   b) With the interior, it will be wise to shoot multiple angles of every room in the house, ensuring to photograph the roof as well as the floor.

   c) You will need to photograph the basement or utility room. Shoot from several angles here. In addition, you need to take pictures of the electrical panel, furnace, and hot water tank. Simply put, we are saying that you should take pictures of just about everything except the seller herself.

d) When shooting the pictures, have the seller accompany you. Ask her lots of probing questions all while keeping yourself busy with the camera. Your being busy will put her at ease and remove the interrogation aspect from the entire prospect. All your questions should lead to finding a definitive answer on the owner's primary motivation for selling. Remember that any information you get will help you negotiate the deal.

When done inspecting the property, and you have determined that it indeed meets your criteria, tell the seller that you will get back to her with an offer the next day. Always make sure to give her a specific date lest she seeks out someone else (when you gain more experience, you may well be able to make an offer on the spot).

Head back to your office and calculate your offer. If you're not well experienced with determining amounts, let this be your guide.

Your offer (also known as a ***maximum allowable offer***), will see you take 70% off the value of the property AFTER repairs, and then subtract the rehab costs and desired assignment fee from it. The final figure will be your ideal amount to offer: the ***Maximum Allowable Offer.*** Use this formula until you are comfortable making deals on the spot.

As you work towards giving the seller a deal, make sure to help the seller while seeking to help yourself.

THE PENULTIMATE WHOLESALING GOAL: SEEK TO HELP YOUR SELLER AS YOU SEEK TO HELP YOURSELF

If you look through Book 1, you will see its insistence on ethical behavior (in the section on legal and illegal aspects of wholesaling). This section echoes the ethical lessons taught in that section.

Too many wholesalers only care about making money and finalizing deals as quickly as possible before moving on to the next one. This is regardless of whether they burn bridges with the seller/buyer or not; to them, nothing matters more than making some bucks. In many instances, such wholesalers fail to experience real success.

A wholesaler with the utmost professionalism works his or her hardest to not only make money but also build a reputation and build bridges. They know that there is nothing more powerful than an endorsement from sellers they have dealt with. When you deal fairly with a motivated seller who is under pressure to sell, he or she will remember and endorse you every chance he or she gets.

Understanding and Sympathizing With the Motivated Seller

Motivated sellers are rarely on a winning streak. Usually, they are facing hardships that are severe enough to prompt them into selling their house. This is why your penultimate goal, even as you seek to make money, is to help them. The question you might have is; how do you do that?

Earning the seller's trust

As a wholesaler, you must earn the seller's trust. Most wholesalers will assure the seller that they are purchasing the house themselves. However, it might be a better idea to tell the motivated seller what is really going on:

1) Tell the motivated seller that your specialty is solving problems for sellers who need to sell quickly.

2) Tell the seller that you have the resources to HELP them and the necessary contacts to make a quick close.

3) Tell the seller that you will do your best to find a genuine and willing buyer. Do not make the mistake so many amateurs make: that of telling the seller that a sale will undoubtedly come through. Let the seller know that while you hold your sales ability in high regard, it is quite possible that the house will not sell before the purchase contract expires.

4) However, even as you are doing your best, to be honest, and straightforward, make sure not to confuse the seller. Tell the seller to trust you and your way of doing things. Do not expose too much of your avenues; you want to seem as invulnerable as possible without being dishonest about it so that the seller can have maximum trust in you.

Assuming that you've succeeded in getting the seller to trust you and have landed a deal, next, we will focus on how to market the contract that's in your hands to increase the likelihood of selling.

MARKETING WHOLESALE PROPERTY DEALS WITH PROSPECTIVE INVESTORS

The number one reason why you and many other wholesalers may find it hard to close wholesaling deals is overpricing your deals

Imagine you have succeeded at getting a house under contract. You are excited and nervous at the same time, and you understand that it's of paramount importance that you close the deal not just because you intend to make money off it, but because you took on the responsibility of getting the job done and are determined to see it through. You know that the seller is relying on you and you want to do everything in your power to cause a few problems as possible.

Pricing Your Deal Too High and Reasons Why You May Do This

This is mostly the major reason why so many wholesalers, especially those new to the business, fail to find a buyer for their deal. You best believe that every house flipper or cash buyer you approach know that you stand to make money from the deal and that the price you offer him or her is higher than the one you offered the seller.

For the most part, they are okay with you trying to make some coin but when the pricing gets absurd, they will turn your nose up to it (you will also draw a similar reaction, by default this time, if every property you have to offer is terrible or always comes with a batch of problems).

Let us examine some reasons why you may feel compelled to overprice your deal or may otherwise overprice your wholesale deal unknowingly.

1: You overestimate your ARV (After Repair Value)

This is often a problem for wholesalers who are working with limited information (also known as wholesalers who insist they do not need many photographs for accurate number crunching, later on). It is also a problem for wholesalers who do not have similar properties on the market for apt comparison. Some wholesalers also act from a place of too much optimism, which is frankly the silliest reason out of the three given in this paragraph. Regardless, every time your ARV is too high, it will follow that you will price your deal too high in turn.

Here is how you can avoid this:

a) Always ensure that for every property you are trying to wholesale, you have similar properties to compare with. Do all you can to find a close match: trawl the web, make phone calls, or drive for dollars if you must.

b) Ensure you have sufficient data from which to estimate your ARV. You can ensure this by arming yourself with lots of photographs that show every angle of the property.

c) Make sure you have recent data to work from. This guide recommendation is that the data you are using be no more than three months old. This is why this book insists on you visiting the property, taking lots of photographs, and asking the seller questions that will guide you to his or her true reasons for wanting to sell.

Here is something else to keep in mind: if you have a tendency to conduct wishful thinking while on business, something often motivated by a desire to make even more money on your deals, you will be better off dumping this trait. Do not play mental games with yourself thinking that because your property has an attractive mural drawing on one of the bedroom walls, you can ask for an extra $5,000 in comparison to what similar properties are going for. Real estate never works this way.

2: You underestimate the rehab work necessary

This one is also all too common. This one is often a result of inexperience in rehab work and determination of repair costs. Sometimes, it is also a result of wishful thinking on the wholesaler's part.

Experienced wholesalers have admitted to routine amazement from the numbers given for repair costs on some wholesale deals they come across. Some of them have admitted to "just going ahead and doubling the amount mentioned for repairs."

Once you underestimate the costs of the rehab work necessary, it follows that you will give an overpriced figure for property in worse shape than you believe it is.

Do you want to know the best way to have an accurate feel for the cost of repairs? Well, ask an experienced real estate investor—you should have several connections by now; he or she will let you know. If you can especially speak to an experienced house flipper, doing so will do you much good. If you cannot find one you can take to lunch and ask questions, your next best option is a contractor. It's wise to find a contractor who has worked for multiple investors (think landlords, house flippers, and the like). Such contractors have their hand on the pulse on repair costs since they are actively involved in the repairs themselves.

3: Your asking wholesale fee is too high

If there ever was a hard and fast rule that ensured longevity in the wholesale business, it is this: ***Do not be greedy.***

At times, you will be tempted to ask for the world because you feel like you spent ages finding the deal and deserve a hefty reward for your troubles. It will be foolhardy to allow emotional rationalization to affect your pricing. The thing to note here is that you want people begging for your deals. You want house flippers calling you constantly to ask if you have anything in your pipeline. The last thing you want is people looking at you as a person who is constantly insulting their intelligence.

It may be difficult for you eat some humble pie and lower your overpriced figure but doing so may be utterly necessary. Even then, there are flippers and cash buyers who would have been willing to buy it at the lower price, if you had priced it that way from the very beginning, who will ignore the lowered price and shun your deals altogether. Avoid greed and always try to price your wholesale fee reasonably.

In the next chapter, we will be looking at real estate laws and what you need to be aware of as you wholesale property.

FOUR THINGS EVERY WHOLESALER SHOULD UNDERSTAND ABOUT REAL ESTATE LAWS

This section continues your education on the legal aspect of wholesaling and real estate. It is necessary that you learn as much as you can about real estate law because the truth is that the more you know about it, the less susceptible you are to breaking it and having to pay costly fines for your mistakes.

Here are four things that as a wholesaler, you ought to understand about real estate laws:

1: In some jurisdictions, the tenant has right of first refusal

When it comes to rental properties, wholesaling is at times not as simple and direct as it is when dealing with residential property. In some jurisdictions, if you are interested in wholesaling a property, you MUST give the tenants who occupy the property the opportunity to match the selling price and purchase the property. Sure enough, this is not something that applies everywhere in the U.S. but some localities demand it.

When dealing with rental property, ensure you are completely familiar with how the law works in your area of interest and whether the Tenant's Right of First Refusal applies in that particular jurisdiction. An attorney will you make sure you are compliant with the rules in place.

2: If you download any forms from the internet, have your local attorney review them before using them

This nugget of advice applies to the forms provided in this book even though they will be as valid as can be. Why is this necessary? Real estate law tends to vary, sometimes greatly, from one jurisdiction to the next. For instance, some jurisdictions will insist on certain languages for certain contracts. Here is an example that depicts what we mean by this:

Many wholesalers love wholesaling leases with the option to buy. This is fine in multiple jurisdictions until you get to Maryland. In Maryland, a lease option MUST mention "THIS IS NOT A CONTRACT TO BUY." If the form does not include this particular "language," any individual involved who did not draft the contract has the right to void it at any time. A lot of the time, this means you will be on the losing end. It is therefore vital to have a local attorney go through your downloaded contract forms to see if they adhere to local law.

If you want, you can skip the downloading bit and use forms drafted by a local attorney specializing in real estate. This will cost you a little bit of money, but that is money well spent because it will ensure your maximum protection.

3: Actual consideration needs to get paid for earnest money deposits & assignments

What does this mean? Well, when you put up a property contract as a wholesaler, you need to pay an "earnest money deposit." Book 1 covers this. An earnest money deposit shows that you and the seller have a deal in place. It serves as evidence of the existence of a real deal between the wholesaler and the seller, thus giving legal credence to all other relative proceedings that develop.

However, problems often arise when the wholesaler and the seller decide to go the "lawyer fee way," by having a nominal fee of, say, $1 or $10 stand in for the requisite earnest money deposit. The thing here is this; a lawyer is a professional, schooled formally in the facets of his or her profession. His schooling guarantees that you cannot exploit or unfairly treat him unless he or she wills it. If the lawyer sees it fit to accept an upfront fee of just $1, the court is alright with it as long as the fee is present whatever it is.

However, unlike the attorney, your seller will not be a legal professional 99% of the time and a court of equity will be compelled to step in if it determines that you are not handling the contract on serious term or there is unfair treatment of the seller. If you pay your seller $10 or even $50 as your earnest money deposit for property that may sell for $70,000, you are begging the equity court to void your contract and being more than a little unprofessional.

Do not be cheap, which means you should never insist on paying a minimal amount. Recall that this book has already insisted that your penultimate goal is to help your motivated seller even as you seek to make money. There often needs to be sufficient consideration money paid to prove that indeed, the deal is real.

4: A title attorney or title company that works with wholesalers is a necessity

No, this does not mean you should set up a fake title company or hire a stand-in title attorney as a smokescreen just because the law asks it. Many wholesalers do this and it eventually comes back to haunt them.

Here is why you need to work with a title company, or at least a title attorney that specializes in working with wholesalers:

As a wholesaler, the motivated buyer is your no. 1 target. In most cases, this automatically means the bulk of properties you are going after are distressed properties that have underlying issues prompting their sale. Each distressed property will likely come with its own unique batch of problems, distressed people, and circumstances.

It could be that the person selling the property is masquerading as the real owner. It could be that there are aliens on the property who have refused to leave the property for years and you do not know about it. You could be dealing with a case of a missing heir or multiple unknown heirs who lay claim to the property.

Best believe that these issues only compound when you attempt to sell off these distressed properties. If you employ a title company or a title attorney, they will help you navigate such issues and warn you if they think the situation warrants pulling the plug.

Let's take the legal discussion a bit further.

A FURTHER EXAMINATION OF THE LEGAL AND ILLEGAL ASPECTS OF WHOLESALING

In this section, we shall outline foolproof strategies that will help you keep on the right side of things as a wholesaler:

Building on Book 1's coverage of the same topic, this section—as was the case in book 1—covers some legal elements of wholesaling. This is important because of way too many wholesalers, especially those relatively new to the business, often get themselves into trouble with the law because they jump straight into wholesaling without necessarily understanding if some of the things they do are legal or not.

With regard to the legal side of things, Book 1 concentrates on the ethics of business: which factors qualify your wholesaling deal as either ethical or unethical regardless of the purity of your intentions. Book 1 mentions dealing with naïve or low-income sellers as unethical and thus, illegal. □

Certainly, it would be unreasonable for your State to demand that you only deal with high-income sellers; the State knows this. However, depending on how you hammer the deal out (with buying at a very low price and proceeding to sell high as an example), the state could find you guilty and penalize you heavily.

This section builds upon Book 1's ethical business coverage (chapter 2), even as it focuses away from it and onto the more technical aspects (meaning that the content here is in no way a substitute for what you learned in book 1. You still have to tend to business ethics first). By saying this section shall concentrate on the "more technical aspects," we primarily mean the brokering issue.

You could be as ethical as ever, you could do business the right way and painstakingly build your portfolio the way a serious wholesaler would and the State could still criminalize your activity and slap you with a penalty on an illegal brokering charge.

Read on to understand this.

The Legality of Wholesaling

Many people who want to put you off wholesaling—usually for their own personal reasons—will repeatedly bash the legality of wholesaling and do all they can to make it seem as if the entire practice is skating on the edge of legality in every aspect of it. Some criticism is valid especially seeing how wholesalers all over the US, with Ohio based ones making up most of the numbers, have had to pay fines for "illegal practices." However, the legality (or lack of) of wholesaling is often exaggerated and there is a lot of nonsense floating around.

Let us determine clearly what is illegal and what is all right for you to do.

What Is Illegal About Wholesaling? The Brokering Issue

The essence of the "is wholesaling really legal?" argument 100% revolves around one term *"brokering."* Different states define the broker in different ways but generally, a broker is the person who helps put a deal together.

Let us delve a bit deeper into this and use Florida's in-depth definition of what a broker is as an example:

Florida states, 'Broker' refers to:

"An individual who, for another individual, and for a compensation or some other valuable consideration, directly or indirectly promised or paid, expressly or impliedly, or with intent to collect or receive a compensation or a valuable consideration, therefore, appraises auctions, sells, exchanges, purchases, rents or offers...to appraise, negotiate the sale or auction the sale, purchase or exchange property...or any interest that concerns the same."

While this definition is longwinded, it drives the point home. Which brings us to this: the people who argue that wholesaling is illegal do so on the claim that the wholesaler is acting in a "broker's capacity" without possessing a license to act in that particular capacity.

A further bump in the situation

To complicate our situation further, there is the problematic issue of "marketing" a property you are not in ownership of. Most states in the U.S insist that "marketing property" qualifies as brokering. Let us go back to our story in Book 1, about James the wholesaler getting a call from Nora the seller, signing a purchase contract with her, assigning the contract to his friend Joe the house flipper and making $5,000 in wholesale fees at the end of it all.

If James did not have Joe as a valuable contact and had put the house up on, say, Craigslist, would he have been marketing Nora's property? You bet he would have! But then again, what if he was not really marketing the property? What defines marketing in the first place? Looking back at our story, do James' approach of Joe, the cash buyer, and house flipper qualify as marketing? If you were to pose this question to 10 different licensed lawyers, you may very well get ten different answers and leave even more confused than before.

What is our take on this? It is indeed true that the way most wholesalers work has illegal elements to it.

Illegal wholesaling

When you put a deal under contract (see purchase agreement) going ahead and telling the world about it on Craigslist and related sites, then going ahead to assign the deal (see assignment agreement) will no doubt get you slapped with a state government fine along with a misdemeanor charge.

What you can do

This chapter will show you several strategies to apply to ensure you do not run afoul of the law. However, always lead your every wholesaling activity with this:

"How comfortable am I if I have to defend my position if my local real estate commission starts asking questions?"

Strategies to Apply to Ensure You Wholesale "The Right Way"

Here are the promised strategies:

1) Get your license: This one does not need too much examination. Nobody will accuse you that you are brokering without the required license if you already

have a license. It may cost you $2,000 but this is far better than having to pay a State penalty for breaking the law.

2) Buy the property and then proceed to sell it: Note that you do not have to do this but it is effective. This way, when you do market your property in whatever capacity you choose to, nobody will accuse you of breaking any law or brokering in any sort of way.

Wholesaling and the Law

The truth is that there is no one answer as far as the legality of wholesaling is concerned. If you do not care about how close to the line you skate, wholesaling is a nice way to make money.

However, to ensure you are operating a wholesaling business that is pure and as solidly legal as it gets, the best strategy that will save you lots of money—in having to buy the property outright before selling it or having to pay a State fine at some point down the line—is to **get your broker's license.** This way, you will completely shut down any claims that you are "brokering without the required license".

In the next chapter, we will be discussing how to conduct contract assignment in the right way.

CONDUCTING CONTRACT ASSIGNMENT THE RIGHT WAY FOR EXAMPLE CONTRACTS EVERY WHOLESALER NEEDS

By now, you may have sat through enough get-rich-quick pitches to know that when it comes to wholesaling, contract assignment is extremely vital. The get-rich-quick gurus do contract assignment introductions all the time, only they never take you through the process as well as all the necessary contracts you need. This section will show you what these "gurus" mean when they say, "You stand to make $5,000 in 30 days via wholesaling contract assignment."

In which scenario will contract assignment be necessary?

We'll keep this simple and terse since Book 1 covers this particular bit competently. A contract assignment will be necessary *"when you find a property owner who is willing to sell their property below its market value. You will then resell the property to another person, often another real estate investor at a higher price."* A contract assignment has the seller commit to selling to you and once he or she puts down a signature, he or she cannot change his or her mind or opt to sell to another person behind your back.

How Does Contract Assignment Work Exactly?

Here is how contract assignment work:

Step 1: Find a motivated seller

We have already explored the concept of the motivated seller. To add some more body to it, a motivated seller is somebody who NEEDS to sell his or her property because of some distress or other aspects of life that precipitates the sale of the property.

Understand that there is a massive disparity between wanting to sell and needing to sell. When an individual "wants" to sell, it is likely that there is no real sense of urgency. The seller may say something like, "I'm curious to see what this house goes for in the current market, since I may well need to sell next year." This sort of fellow is not a motivated seller. On the other hand, somebody who "needs" to sell is often conducting a running battle against time and is likely to say something like, "I have to sell my property ASAP as I am moving back to Alabama to nurse my ailing father."

Step 2: Get an assignment contract signed by both you and the seller

Multiple assignment contracts are available on the internet (and this book will give you several you can photocopy and use.) However, and this very book has insisted on it in a previous section, you need to ensure a local attorney goes through your contract template to ensure it's in line with the laws in your particular jurisdiction.

Both you and the seller need to sign the assignment contract. This contract, in addition to having the seller commit to only selling to you, empowers you to "assign" the purchase to a 3rd party, and as you well understand by now, your wholesaling career will make absolutely no sense without the presence of this 3rd party.

Step 3: Submit the contract to title

This process tends to differ by state. Still, there is not much by way of intricacies or complexities. Whichever state you operate from, you deal with a closing attorney or a title company. Most states will let you choose whomever you fancy dealing with. Take care to understand the stipulations of your state regarding this.

The Title Company or closing attorney will conduct a title search to verify that the seller is a valid one. The title search checks the property's historical records—to ensure there are no "aliens" on the property—and a host of other things. If the title company concludes that the property has a "defective title," which essentially means that the ownership of the property is not straightforward and complicates any buying/selling procedures, it is wise to let the property go and look for something else.

The title search is a necessary process because most distressed properties often have a lot of baggage. Do not be one of those wholesalers who are too cheap or too impatient to see this process through or someone who is too foolish to understand that a title search is only in place to protect them.

Step 4: Find a buyer and assign the contract assignment to him/her

As you get started out in this business, finding a buyer may be quite daunting. However, you will get one eventually, provided the property you have on your hands is not so bad to a point of being unsellable. When you get a buyer, you can then begin your process of completing the transaction and the whole business altogether. Assign the contract to the buyer and sign a purchase agreement to finalize everything.

However, how do you ensure that your buyer is actually serious? How do you ensure that he or she is not just poking around for a prospective property that he or she "could buy some unspecified time in the future when the money or circumstances are right?" To ensure you are dealing with a solid buyer, you should insist on a non-refundable "earnest money deposit" fee.

Having the buyer furnish this amount will solidify your position as far as making a profit goes. It does not matter if the buyer ends up buying the property or backs out at the last moment; this money will remain yours. This amount may be as much or as little as you require; just keep it reasonable and you will be fine. (Most wholesalers prefer several hundreds of dollars, but some seasoned ones will ask for as much as $5,000). When the buyer deposits this amount, you can be sure that he or she is interested in buying the property.

NOTE: Your title company or closing attorney will hold this fee until the completion of the transaction/deal or until the buyer backs out.

Step 5: Get Paid

This is the wholesaler's favorite part. You will typically make your money/get paid once the end buyer wires the funds for your deal. As outlined before, this money will cover the amount you agreed with the original property seller as well as your amount for facilitating the whole thing (wholesale fee).

Examples of Necessary Contracts Every Wholesaler Needs

As stated earlier, you need several contracts as you embark on wholesaling. The most important ones you need are:

Sample Assignment Contract

This is a sample assignment contract you can tweak and make yours. Remember to have an attorney look it over to ensure its regality in your state (do this for all the contracts here)

Agreement for Sale Contract

To ensure you get a contract that is nicely formatted, you can download one from this link:

https://www.dropbox.com/s/d87nyy7ql4k9t21/AGREEME NT%20FOR%20SALE%20Contract.doc?dl=0:

Sample Purchase Agreement 1

This link has a customizable sample purchase agreement:

https://www.dropbox.com/s/8zbyt0gz50eeanl/Purchase%2 0and%20Sale%20Agreement.doc?dl=0

Sample Purchase Agreement 2

This link has another customizable purchase agreement:

https://www.dropbox.com/sh/diqx90c07ens4hj/AACod1W 4GpyO0NGype59RvRaa?dl=0

Sample Purchase Agreement 3

This link has a standard purchase and sale agreement:

https://www.dropbox.com/s/3w095rel7ylgn98/Standard% 20Purchase%20and%20Sale%20Agreement.doc?dl=0

Option to Purchase Agreement

Here is a sample option to purchase agreement:

https://www.dropbox.com/s/admnnk2pa827ky3/Option%2 0to%20Purchase%20Agreement.doc?dl=0

Option to Purchase (Flex Option) Agreement

https://www.dropbox.com/s/yol7f6oqx47gqqc/Option%20t o%20Purchase%20Real%20Estate%20Agreement.doc?dl=0 has another option to purchase agreement that you can customize

To take it even a bit further, here (https://www.dropbox.com/s/qc3tqw7n2whc8sn/Sample% 20Contract%20Assignment%20with%20Specific%20Details .doc?dl=0) is a sample contract assignment with specific details, dates, and monetary figures.

You can download the templates from this link:

https://www.dropbox.com/sh/diqx9oco7ens4hj/AACod1W 4GpyOoNGype59RvRaa?dl=0

Last but not least, we will discuss something very critical in wholesaling.

YOUR SELLER LEAD SHEET: WHAT TO SAY WHEN YOUR PHONE RINGS AND THERE'S A CUSTOMER ON THE LINE

You know what a motivated seller is and even more importantly, you know how to seek out their business. If you follow everything outlined in this book, there will come a time when you have no problems drawing in customers and pushing multiple deals.

With this said, what do you do when the big moment arrives and the phone rings with a motivated seller on the line? You may be asking yourself any of the following questions:

1. What shall I say to the customer?

2. How do I conduct myself so that I inspire confidence in him or her?

3. What are the questions that I should ask?

4. What will come next even if I do everything right?

This section will help you not just assess incoming real estate seller leads, but turn them into viable opportunities:

1: Remember that a motivated seller requires your help often more than you need his/hers.

When a motivated seller goes out of her way to call you, it is usually the case that she needs your help and would appreciate it if you helped her move her property as fast as possible. This is why the first thing to do before picking up your phone is to breathe deeply and calm yourself down. If you are nervous and shifty and the motivated seller, who may possess the very same emotions, catches on, she will lose her confidence in you from the start and immediately consider seeking out somebody else.

Just relax, breathe deeply, and pick up your phone. If a motivated seller is on the line, something you will know soon enough by her attitude and particular situation, you will have a deal in little time. Otherwise, if it is not a motivated seller on the line, bid them goodbye and hang up. Many new wholesalers make the mistake of trying to convince a seller to make a fast sale. As a wholesaler, remember that your job is not to create urgency; your job is to act upon present urgency in your seller.

2: With the pleasantries covered, employ a set of questions on the seller

Not only will this help you keep the conversation going, and thus put the seller at ease, it will also help you glean vital information about the seller so that you have a clear picture on who you are dealing with.

Here are the things to ask about:

1. The details of the property for sale (number of bathrooms, bedrooms, address Etc.)

2. The primary reason for selling

3. What he or she believes the house is worth at least based on similar sales in their neighborhood

4. The asking price, if they already have one in mind, and whether they would consider lowering it

5. The repairs and rehab activities the house needs

It is vital to remember that you should not take a seller's word as fact until you have visited the house. A distressed seller eager to sell quickly may exaggerate some things and gloss over others. Still, never underestimate the importance of building rapport. Humans tend to do business with other humans they like. Rather than sound too formal or professional, be warm and walk the customer through your questions as you would an old friend. In other words, be casual all through.

3: Assess the customer's need level

As you walk the customer through your questions, pay great attention to the signals he or she sends:

1. What is the true reason behind the sale?

2. Is the need immediate?

3. How much money are they really looking for?

Getting answers to these questions will greatly help you understand whether you want to go ahead with the deal on the table or not. If, for instance, your customer starts talking about all the recent upgrades made to their house, understand that such a seller stands a better chance of getting top dollar with an agent and politely end the conversation.

4: *A confident person will speak directly and give confident answers*

This bit will glue together everything else on this section and determine the level of success you have in inspiring the seller's confidence. Many wholesalers concern themselves with whether (or not) they will come across as nervous. Will the customer detect nervousness or inexperience?

A simple strategy to exude both confidence and professionalism is to speak in a calm voice. Keep your words plain as well. When your answers are short, simple, and straight to the point, you will usually sound like a person who knows his business.

For example, let us assume that you've found direct mail to be the best approach to generating leads and the seller asks how you got their name. Your best answer would be, "I purchased an address list based on tax records."

The seller could as well ask about your particular interest in his or her property. You do not need to make your answer complicated or use too many words to try to impress. You may simply say, "I purchase houses in my neighborhood and rehabilitate them. After I am through with that, I either sell them or rent them out." This is a simple yet honest answer.

Most property owners understand that rehabilitating and selling off properties is something some real estate investors do. However, avoid describing yourself as an "investor." It may come across as entitled and lacking in humility.

5: Do not be afraid to ask for a little time if you need it

Many wholesalers assume that they have to know the answers to everything upfront. It is not your job to know everything even though it helps to be knowledgeable. If the customer asks you a question and you are unsure of the correct answer, just let such a customer know you will seek out the necessary information and call back with an answer. Again, keep it simple and be calm. A lot of the time, calm and simple is all you need to gain your customer's trust.

CONCLUSION

We have come to the end of the book. Thank you for reading and congratulations on reading until the end.

At this point, you can call yourself a competent wholesaler. Both Book 1 and this one have done a superb job of showing you how to conduct business as a pro wholesaler. There is a fair share of unconventional advice within, and it is my recommendation that you take everything here to heart.

Remember that wholesaling is something anyone can do. It does not matter whether you have a million dollars in the bank or not; it does not matter if your family has a track record of real estate success or not; all that matters is that you are willing to put in the work. This book guides you steadily- by getting to this point, you have already learned all the important elements of wholesaling. You are ready to be a successful wholesaler.

However, with wholesaling being such a vast topic, it is impossible for two books to cover everything. You will still need to glean as much as you can from other sources. However, this book is more than good enough as a spine for your wholesaling education.

If you found the book valuable, can you recommend it to others? One way to do that is to post a review on Amazon.

Please leave a review for this book on Amazon!

Thank you and good luck!

ERNIE BRAVEBOY

REAL ESTATE MARKETING HOW TO BE A REAL-ESTATE MILLIONAIRE

ERNIE BRAVEBOY

INTRODUCTION

I want to thank you and congratulate you for buying the book, *"Real Estate Marketing How to Be a Real-Estate Millionaire"*.

This book has actionable information on how to become a real estate millionaire by marketing real estate like a pro.

Real estate is undoubtedly one of the most stable investment vehicles world over. This explains why almost every billionaire has interests in real estate. Luckily, with real estate, you don't have to be a billionaire or millionaire to get started; you can make money with real estate without owning any property!

How is that so? Well, you can do that by being a real estate agent, marketer, flipping houses, wholesaling and much, much more. The good news is that you can make thousands of dollars per deal, which puts you on a very unique position to make millions of dollars a year.

And if you are looking for comprehensive information on how to make a million dollars as a real estate agent, this book has all you need to follow to get there. In this book, you will discover what it takes to be a real estate marketer, the different ways in which you can make money and how you can actually make money from being a real estate marketer. Whether you are a real estate agent, wholesaler, flipper or homeowner looking to sell your property, you will find this book very helpful in ensuring you close a deal fast. Let's begin.

ERNIE BRAVEBOY

Thanks again for buying this book. I hope you enjoy it!

REAL ESTATE MARKETING: A BACKGROUND

Marketing is at the core of real estate; it is the fuel that drives real estate. Think about it; whether you are an agent, developer, a wholesaler, a flipper or a homeowner wishing to sell, rent out or lease out your property, you MUST unleash the full power of marketing to generate leads and ultimately attract customers who are willing and able to pay the selling price or the rent amount. However, the purpose of this book is not just about selling property one off; it is about making a business out of it so that you can sell to all types of customers repeatedly.

The thing with real estate marketing is that it has to be continual; you don't just do it once then sit back to get people desperately looking for your property to rent/buy. It is just like any other worthwhile course like losing weight; you really don't expect that exercising once and eating the right foods once will make you lose 10 pounds instantly irrespective of how extreme your measures are. You have to commit to eating right and exercising if you are keen on making any significant progress over time. Similarly, with real estate, you must market effectively and consistently to see any real progress.

The question is; how can you do it effectively to a point of being able to make millions of dollars from your craft?

Well, that's what we will get straight into starting with the first step i.e. finding property that you will be marketing because when you think about it, if you have no property to market, you have no business being a real estate marketer.

Note: Keep in mind that I already stated that with real estate marketing, you don't have to own the property that you are marketing. Let's begin there.

STEP 1: FIND PROPERTY TO SELL: HOW TO FIND THE BEST SELLERS

There are many ways to find sellers of real estate, and anyone will tell you to check the newspaper ads, buy leads from websites, put up signs inscribed 'we are buying houses', sending advertisements and so on. I'm sure you know about these strategies and even more.

Most of these strategies are okay and will get you real estate property. However, my strategy is different. I don't just look for sellers; I look for the best sellers and the best sellers according to me are:

1. People who are willing to sell their property for a low price, a very low price; this generally means selling it somewhere between 10% - 30% of market value. Sounds impossible I know, but it's not.

2. Again, the best sellers are people willing to sell their property with flexible terms. This means that I'm targeting a seller who will accept to finance the property for you, require no cash down and also charge no interest (0% interest).

As you will soon note, our aim is coming up with a list of the prospective sellers and mailing them immediately, this is how you do it:

Begin by finding a targeted list of various property owners who are extremely motivated to actually sell. Ideally, you aren't looking for just every list of property owners; you are looking for very specific property owners who are more likely to sell their property than the usual owner. We have a number of ways to go about acquiring these lists and obviously, some methods can work better than others depending on your area.

The first option: Work with the county

In this case, you'll be looking for your county's delinquent tax list. This is a list you will not lack in every county and this list always contains a goldmine of info that can assist you to pin down some of the most motivated sellers in your locality.

NOTE: A city, township or county keeps a detailed record of every property within its area of jurisdiction to be able to charge taxes effectively. This means that they have information on the following:

- The property's owner

- How much is paid for the property

- How much the owner owes in taxes

Among other details

All this info is in the public records and thus, you can find this data on any property you want in the US. Most county websites will provide this information for free even though sometimes their systems tend to be confusing to work with. Luckily, we have other services such as; agentpro 247 (discussed in the next point) that will provide about the same data, only in a package that's easier to understand. For example:

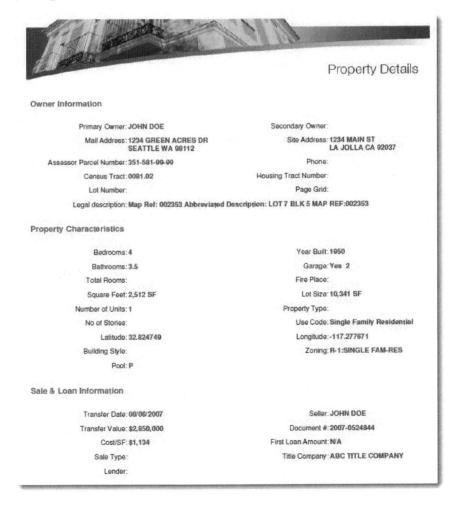

Property Details

Owner Information

Primary Owner: JOHN DOE

Mail Address: 1234 GREEN ACRES DR
SEATTLE WA 98112

Assessor Parcel Number: 351-581-99-99

Census Tract: 0081.02

Lot Number:

Secondary Owner:

Site Address: 1234 MAIN ST
LA JOLLA CA 92037

Phone:

Housing Tract Number:

Page Grid:

Legal description: Map Ref: 002353 Abbreviated Description: LOT 7 BLK 5 MAP REF:002353

Property Characteristics

Bedrooms: 4

Bathrooms: 3.5

Total Rooms:

Square Feet: 2,512 SF

Number of Units: 1

No of Stories:

Latitude: 32.824749

Building Style:

Pool: P

Year Built: 1950

Garage: Yes 2

Fire Place:

Lot Size: 10,341 SF

Property Type:

Use Code: Single Family Residential

Longitude: -117.277671

Zoning: R-1:SINGLE FAM-RES

Sale & Loan Information

Transfer Date: 08/06/2007

Transfer Value: $2,850,000

Cost/SF: $1,134

Sale Type:

Lender:

Seller: JOHN DOE

Document #: 2007-0524844

First Loan Amount: N/A

Title Company: ABC TITLE COMPANY

(You can thus use the service when you find difficulty employing this method.)

Therefore, when property owners fail to pay their taxes, the county treasurer creates a running list of such people-which is basically the same list the county uses to mail out the delinquent tax notices.

You have to note that there are many people in this list who will be very willing to sell their property at a very steep discount- and most of them rarely want to advertise their desperation. They need somebody like you to 'help' them and make the whole process idiot-proof.

It is not always easy to get this information though- you have to expect the list to cost you something. Most county treasurers might charge you something to give you the list.

The good thing about this method is that you always get fresh and accurate data because anyway, it is coming from the database in real time.

The second option: Working with a data provider

You can also get this list from a data service dealing with real estate.

We have numerous data companies that can give you these lists in a clean and workable format. While some are expensive, some are reasonably cheap and if you understand what type of property you are looking for, your search might end here.

These data companies comb through almost all the counties in the United States and make it very easy to find property.

Let's take one example:

AgentPro247

AgentPro247 is a service that offers public record information. This means that you can actually look up any property in a few minutes and find the info you need.

This service is one of the easiest to use, to sign up and offers one of the best property research tools you can ever find. Unlike the counties, it is not just about the lists but also about the ease of the due diligence process, especially for niche property types like vacant land.

One thing I appreciate about this service is that their system informs you just how current their database is in each county in the country.

Other data providers providing that could assist you in a similar way to get this list include the following:

- ReboGateway

- RealQuest

- Melissa Data

- ListSource

You job now is to use the data provider to target or sort lists based on these characteristics:

- Out-of-state property owners (those living outside the county): People living out-of-state are usually more disconnected and disengaged from their properties. For whatever reason, many of them had to move away unexpectedly and chances are they have a vested interest in liquidating as soon as they can.

Other characteristics you might want to consider include:

- Absentee owners or people who aren't living in their property

- Property owners who've owed their property for ten or more years

- Property owners with delinquent taxes

- Properties in good price range

Send the message

Once you pull your list and sort it out, the next step is sending the mail to the owner. The process of doing so can be simple or difficult, depending on the method- for instance, if you've ever tried putting together a bulk mail campaign on your own before, you must know how dreary it can be. This is why we have to use Click2Mail.

Click2Mail is a service that can allow you upload your pre-sorted list, your postcard template and send your bulk email campaigns without any production work needed. It will print, stamp and mail everything for you and charge postage rates and production costs, which are typically lower than you would otherwise incur if you choose to stamp and mail the postcards in-house. The process is amazingly simple-check out the picture below to learn more.

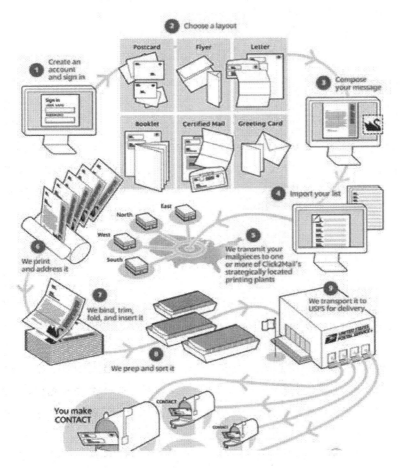

When you contact the recipient and settle on a good deal, it is time to market the property:

- Get to know more about the property so that you are able to sell what you understand in and out.

- Take good pictures and create high quality videos of the property to post on your website to market it as from this point, our focus is on the buyer.

Side note:

Before you start marketing the property though, you have to understand your investment strategy; what kind of a marketer are you? While you will find business people purchasing property and selling it using the 'buy and hold' or flipping techniques, most marketers don't technically own any property; most marketers are largely wholesalers or just plain agents.

Who is a wholesaler?

A wholesaler is a person who looks for good deals in real estate, writes a contract to acquire the deal and then sells that contract to another buyer. This means that the wholesaler doesn't actually own the property he/she is selling but puts a property, say a distressed home, under contract so that he/she assigns that contract to another buyer. The wholesaler then markets the home to prospective buyers for a price higher than they placed the property under contract for. You can therefore view a wholesaler as a person or a middleman who gets money for finding deals. As a wholesaler, you can sell your contract to retail buyers or just sell them to investors (like house flippers) referred to as the 'cash buyers'. When you're dealing with these cash buyers, you get money within weeks or even days and can easily create robust connections in the real estate network. You can read more about wholesaling at https://fitsmallbusiness.com/how-to-wholesale-real-estate/ for more information.

As I stated earlier, you can also choose to become a flipper- a strategy that is not common to folks who've decided to focus on real estate marketing. A flipper purchases real estate property at a discounted price, develops or improves it over time and then sells it for profit. This is similar to the other strategy referred to as 'buy and hold' where the investor buys property and holds it so that he sells it in future for a better price. Between the time of buying and selling, he/she could rent it out to get extra money.

If at all you want to take on any of these investment strategies (apart from being a plain agent/marketer), you might find the first one (wholesaling) more appealing than the rest if you want to mainly focus on being a marketer.

Note:

Ideally, you need to ensure that you make a profit depending on what you do. If you are into flipping, then you have to consider such things like expected cost of repair, your expected profit and the value of property after repair. Using these three will help you to determine the price you should pay for any property on sale to ensure you don't end up burning yourself accidentally. You can use https://investfourmore.com/fix-and-flip-70-percent-rule-calculator/ or http://www.pinefinancialgroup.com/fix-and-flip-calculator-iphone-app/. You can as well use http://www.creditfinanceplus.com/calculators/house-flipping-net-profit.php. You can learn how to determine the value of property after repair using the guidelines https://www.creonline.com/how-to-determine-market-value.html As for determining the expected cost of repair, you can refer to https://www.auction.com/blog/how-to-properly-estimate-repair-costs-on-a-flip/, https://investfourmore.com/2014/11/03/much-cost-fix-repair-house/ and https://patchofland.com/blog/all-projects/2017/04/11/how-to-estimate-repair-costs-accurately-when-flipping-a-property/. Issues to do with the nitty gritties of flipping and wholesaling are really outside the scope of this book. However, the guidelines above will make it very easy for you to follow the whole process with a lot of ease until you find the right property to market.

The truth is; you shouldn't have a hard time finding property to market if you follow the guidelines above. Now that you have property to market, it is time to come up with a clear plan/strategy because as you are well aware, failing to plan/strategize is synonymous with planning/strategizing to fail. That's why the next thing we will be discussing is strategy.

STEP 2: DEVELOP YOUR REAL ESTATE MARKETING STRATEGY

As a real estate marketer, you can go online, stick to the offline methods or use both of them. If you want to incorporate the online tactics, you need to first of all think about real estate marketing that incorporates web design, online lead generation and search marketing among others. Your digital strategy is important all the way through-regardless of the stage of the process you are in (whether pre-development or post-development). Therefore, my assumption is that you already have a website.

Do you have a real estate marketing website?

If you don't, the first thing you should probably do is get a good, topnotch website. You have two options: create one yourself if you have some bit of knowledge of how to go about it or hire a professional to do it for you. You can hire a professional from Fiverr.com, Upwork.com, Guru.com, Freelancer.com or Peopleperhour.com. If you are an intermediate computer user, you can use a website builder like those shown at http://www.top10bestwebsitebuilders.com/comparison

Why is this important?

A few tips...

Potential clients want to work with a person they can trust, a person who's looking out for them and can offer valuable advice along the way. Your website is now your first meet and greet.

The website's content is everything; from headlines to navigation, videos, images, blogs- all the components that tell the story of your brand.

When a visitor lands on your site, they naturally base the quality of your listings and services off what they see; and even though we are often taught not to judge a book by its cover when growing up, in this situation, the cover is everything. Consider that the largest part of this market is visual, so you have to use large, bold and beautiful images. You need to allow your properties to speak for themselves.

Again, we have more and more websites incorporating flat designs and doing away with three dimension elements - they pay attention to flat colors and typography (the styles, colors and fonts that identify your brand). This design gives your site a fresh, modern appearance.

Perhaps you need to also know that today, sites are really growing off responsive background videos and images. You have only a couple of seconds to catch the attention of the user, so showcase your most attractive and desirable properties with beautiful and high resolution visuals.

I really don't consider having a website in this day and age part of a plan; it is a must have so as you start planning, you MUST have the essentials first.

The first strategy is planning. Without it, everything else would be largely unworkable.

NOTE: The steps of the plan as discussed below are only an overview of what you'll do from here. We'll discuss in more detail some important parts of it in the subsequent parts of this book. So don't worry when it all seems too much or complicated to gather.

Create a Marketing Plan

Before the plan can commence, you have to set realistic and specific goals. You need to decide what you really want your real estate marketing endeavors to fulfill as this will help you to set clear expectations for all your social media presence, website, email campaigns, blog, among other tactics to take on.

With the four steps provided below, you will be able to fully plan your real estate marketing strategy.

Outline the 4Ws of real estate marketing

The 4Ws refer to "Who, What, Where and When" which is a good place to start in creating your plan. You can be general at first with the 'Ws' but over time, you can make them more specific. For example, if the idea you have about your general audience is broad (perhaps all sellers in a single community instead of sellers in a specific price bracket), that's okay. You can come back to these Ws and then tweak them accordingly. To get started though, write them down so that you have some understanding of how you'll structure your real estate marketing plan.

From this point onwards, the book will be based on a plan that contains the following milestones and objectives below.

The who: determine your target audience

The when: determine a timetable for success

The where: identify the platforms to take with your marketing

The what: implement your plan and identify the metrics you'll build upon

1: Determine Your Target Audience

Knowing who to market to is important; and forms a big part of the battle. Make sure to target a suitable niche group of purchasers and sellers with whom you have worked in the past or who you'd want to market to. Also, do not worry if you cannot yet isolate an exact demographic you think is best to reach as narrowing your focus even a bit will improve your success greatly.

There's one factor that you need to consider though when selecting a primary audience: think of your past client- if you've had any. If you have not earned much money off a particular segment of sellers and buyers, perhaps you should think about marketing to a new group; but if you're contented with your revenue in the recent months and years, you can keep to marketing to the same audience.

Another factor to consider is the housing market statistics: what do they indicate? Currently, the figures that relate to income, home sales, property values and many other areas greatly have a profound influence on the marketing decisions for brokers and agents throughout the nation. You need to look for this data for your local market to decide the kind of people who are worth pursuing and who are not. For instance, if the statistics indicate that in your community, millennials are purchasing the majority of homes for sale, chances are they would make a good core audience.

2: Determine a Timetable for Success

As you will note, there is not really an exact length of time it takes a professional and brand to see significant results from their marketing efforts. Nonetheless, this does not mean you cannot have specific goals to aim for in the long haul. Take a look at these examples of goals to aspire to after different periods.

- After a month- since your marketing is just getting started or going, you could aim to increase more awareness of your company online. When you gain acknowledgement as a successful real estate firm in your area, it means you are doing very well so far.

- After 3 months- about a quarter into your plan, you could target moderate goals related to social media followers, lead gen, site traffic , general online inquiries from clients and potential new contacts

- After 6 months- after the first year into your strategy, you should have greater ambitions such as getting a particular amount of targeted seller leads or a particular number of closed deals.

It wouldn't do you much good to look out further than a year down the line because it's very difficult to expect what will change over the course of 12 months with your business.

You should thus set goals for the future that can be easily foreseen.

3: Identify the Platforms/Avenues/Tactics to Take With Your Marketing

After knowing your marketing demographic, choose the methods or channels you want to use in order to support your business. Definitely, the core group of tactics such as email, social media blogging and using a website are all the ones you should use from the beginning, but you shouldn't be afraid of trying other useful marketing ploys such as hosting podcasts or webinars, creating infographics and creating long-form content such as reports, e-books and so forth.

You will never know which tactics work best with you unless you try a variety of them. Also don't forget that your website is the foundation of all your marketing activities since your audience is led there by most of your marketing activities- if not all.

We'll go through some of the best marketing methods or avenues you can use but before that, we have to consider something first:

The marketing costs

Before taking up any marketing strategy or tasks, you need to consider the costs involved compared to how much you are willing to spend.

While most marketing tasks require your time, some require a good amount of financial investment as well. You can create blog posts and other written content without spending anything significant- just find stats, news and other information to curate from other publications or simply create 'how-to' articles of your own based on your know-how and experiences- just like that, you have information to share with your audience.

On the other hand, we have the paid campaigns- which is mainly advertising. These require a more detailed plan and money. For the paid advertising efforts, you can take a closer look at your revenue for the past couple of months as well as the much you are expecting to earn in the subsequent months. After that, you can apportion part of this amount for your ad spend. You could use the following paid advertising avenues:

Google AdWords- here, you can efficiently reach a qualified audience by targeting certain keywords.

Facebook AdWords- you'll be offered display ads that can be featured in News Feeds and sides of pages. Advertisements on such a platform provide a unique way to reach your audience in a targeted manner- that is to say, designating exactly who views your advertisement according to demographic criteria such as location, interests and age.

Twitter ads- you can promote your whole twitter account or certain tweets in the same way as Facebook ads. Every so often, Twitter adds new ad options for brands- so you need to research the page- 'Twitter for business' to view the opportunities that could work for you.

Google Display Network ads- while you can create advertisements to appear in the search results for different terms related to your local market and business, you can also aim for certain sites on which to have the ads displayed.

The above examples are part of the online strategies. Offline strategies like using billboards or holding seminars can also cost you more than others like using bandit signs.

NOTE: Whatever the types of ads you choose, you need to do more research on the merits and demerits of each. Either way, you should investigate each ad option- One or more of them could assist you reach buyers and sellers better.

Let's now see examples of tactics you could use to drive people to your website, to give you an idea of where to start if you became absolutely clueless.

STEP 3: TAKING ACTION

Online Strategies

1: Email Marketing

Email marketing is still very effective in our digital world of instant messages, tweets and quick moving news feeds. Therefore, it always works to send interesting, informational and newsworthy newsletters to your sphere of influence because:

People are always checking their email throughout the day and you thus have the opportunity to get yourself into their inbox. The good thing with real estate marketing is that most people will look at houses, as it is very difficult to resist clicking a picture of a beautiful kitchen!

As a rule of thumb, you need to note that many people find their dream home when they aren't looking and thus, a targeted email newsletter is a good way to catch their interest.

So, get started, sign up with an email marketing service such as Mailchimp. You will note that many such companies actually offer a free service, which includes tips and templates on creating and sending a perfect newsletter. You will also be able to monitor your results by seeing the open rate and also the number of people who clicked on links to your listings. You can use these results to inform sellers that their home has been viewed.

Other popular email marketing services include:

AWeber- Its platform is easy to get started with and it also connects to other platforms like WordPress seamlessly. What's more, you are able to access ready to use email templates, autoresponders, email tracking and autoresponders with it.

ConvertKit- this is a strong platform that is commonly used by marketers, authors as well as professional bloggers. It allows you to (among other things) offer content upgrades and incentives together with email signup forms. It also comes with auto-responders that are easy to manage which lets you send drip emails.

GetResponse- highly regarded as one of the top email marketing solutions, GetResponse is easy to use and makes email marketing for fresh startups seem so simple. It has great marketing automation tools that allow you to create smart automated campaigns. You can create campaigns, send content designed for specific groups and segment contacts with a drag and drop builder. These tools are sure to help you create effective campaigns to boost your profits.

Tip:

1. Emails are a great way to get your brand and expertise out there. They can and actually should have up-to-date-listings, but also let folks know you are on top of your game with everything that's going on in the market within your location.

2. Moreover, people are always researching online for homes but when they are selecting an agent, they want a personal connection. If you want to be identified as an

expert in your area, you have to ensure you include local items in your email; list of remarkable hardware stores and nurseries, a detailed review of restaurants, a recommendation for a resident contractor and so on.

Please learn more about how to setup your email marketing program at https://www.campaignmonitor.com/resources/guides/getting-started-with-email-marketing/.

2: *Social Media Engagement*

The different social media platforms are a fantastic way to promote and sell your listings, engage with your followers, grow your network, promote and sell your listings and attract buyers as well as sellers too. Let's take one example:

Facebook

You need to start with your inner circle to build up your network- and Facebook is a great avenue to do that. From my own experience, the people who know about you will easily get excited quickly about your real estate trade as it is a great platform to let people know who you are and there's something fresh and awesome you are doing that should be taken seriously, and also grow your circle of influence at the same time.

Post your videos on your pages, groups, timelines and even inbox your friends directly with the videos and pictures.

Update your occupation, post real estate tips, start real conversations with people about what you've learned and perhaps also where you hope your career will go. It is possible you will like the results even if you only invest a couple of minutes per day.

Other popular platforms include

- LinkedIn

- Tweeter

- Instagram

- Snapchat

- Pinterest

Note: As a real estate agent, you cannot afford not to have a Facebook page because it can help you generate leads for your website and engage prospects with greater ease. And if you could combine it with YouTube and other social medial platforms that use images like Pinterest and Instagram, you will find generate leads with greater ease.

Generally, posting and tweeting your listings gets them viewed by many people and you can include information that might not be shared by a regular newspaper or postcard ad.

The most important thing you have to remember when using social media to market real estate is that it works best when you view and handle it as a two way street. It is imperative you comment, like and share posts of other members (not just focusing on publishing your own). The more engagement your post receives, the more views it receives. Acknowledging other people's comments on your post is also another way to show that you are well engaged in your social media presence which will not only help get your post become viewed by more people, but assist you start a conversation and attract more followers.

3: Paid Advertising/Campaigns

We'll first look at Facebook ads in detail before taking a brief look at Google AdWords.

How to set up Facebook ads

Note: you need to make sure your website is formatted properly so that you don't risk reducing the number of people opting in to your message significantly.

In this regard, there are some things you can do to make your website convert properly.

Not familiar with the term **conversion** *(in websites)?*

Conversion refers to getting your visitors or users to perform what you want-whether it's buying your product, signing up for your newsletter, downloading a whitepaper, registering for a webinar or even filling a lead or contact form. Website conversion is thus most critical factor to the success of online marketing strategy. This is because if your website is to generate any qualified leads, the visitor should be able to open the channels of communication by either subscribing, sharing, saving etc.

Conversion rate on the other hand refers to the percentage of users who take a particular desired action. For instance:

Let's assume your website is visited by 100,000 users during the month of December. And 2000 users purchased or requested to see your property from the site. Thus, the conversion rate of your website is 2% (2,000/100,000)

- Write blogs that are simple to read (at least one for every business day).

In this case, even the titles matter, and since simple word changes can tremendously increase or reduce conversions, companies like Buzzffeed and Groupon spend millions of dollars split testing headlines. You can gain from this for free. Simply go to buzzsumo.com and enter 'real estate'. You will find the most popular articles on real estate on the web- just pick ten titles and begin writing considering that all these titles are all pre-tested. Actually, everything about writing a post has all been laid out for you.

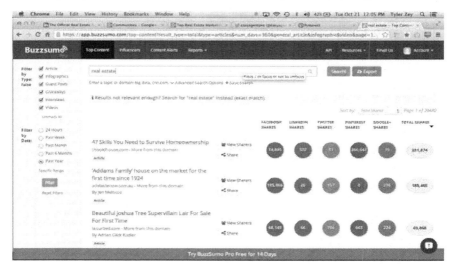

- Each blog requires a graphic to go with it. This makes sure your Facebook ads for real estate convert well.

You can order some graphics from a site like Fiverr.com for as little as $5. Just ensure to look for someone offering 'flat design', as this is a trend that came out not so long ago that gives graphics a very sharp appearance.

NOTE: Good graphics tend to drive people to convert into your email list and actually share their contact.

Conversion techniques

You need ways to drive people to convert onto your email list on your website. I would recommend that you have four different kinds of email capture boxes. Just ensure every one of them is offering something different in exchange for the email address and phone number.

Take the following example:

You can have one landing page containing a capture form and three different forms of opt-in boxes on your site, all of which are making different offers.

A good example of an opt-in box (if you're not familiar with this term):

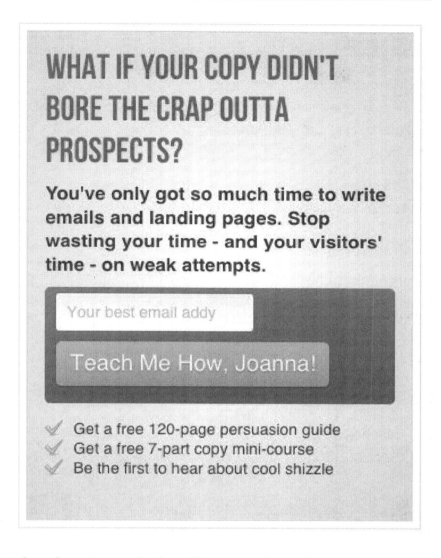

After that, input the headline you chose from Buzzsumo as the headline on the opt-in box or landing page. When someone subscribes to your email list, make sure you send them the free content.

Well, Congratulations! Your site now has great content that people want to read.

My assumption is that at this point, your site is well set up to receive a good number of phone numbers and email addresses from any traffic sent to it. You can prime the site with paid traffic and we're going to do that using Facebook ads so that we get the phone contacts and email addresses.

We are going to start with Facebook ads, which I'll explain how to set up step by step then move on to Google AdWords, which are usually more costly and competitive.

- Choose 3 of your favorite articles you did about your business and head over to the Facebook website.

- Click the button labeled 'manage your ads'.

- Next, go ahead and click 'create ads'.

- After that, choose 'clicks to website'.

- Now enter the URL to the best article you've written on your site.

- The image you designed should appear below. You will want to choose three other images from the stock image library of Facebook. This will assist you split test your ads.

- After that, connect your Facebook page.

- Input the title of your article in the little 'headline' box then write a short description.

- Now turn on the Mobile Newsfeed Ads ad Newsfeed Ads.

- Turn off the Partner Mobile Aps and Sidebar ads because they don't really convert as well when you're running Facebook Ads especially for Real Estate.

Congratulations for completing that part. Let's now discuss how to set up ads for real estate.

I recommend the following demographics:

135

Locations	United States, Missouri
	Kansas City + 25 mi
	Add a country, state/province, city or ZIP
Age	25 ▼ - 55 ▼
Gender	**All** Men Women
Languages	Enter a language...
Relationship Status	**In a relationship** ×
	Married ×
	Engaged ×
	Choose relationship statuses ┊ Browse
Education Level	**College grad** ×
	Associate degree ×
	Choose education statuses ┊ Browse
Income	**Income ($50,000 - $75,000)** ×
	Income ($75,000 - $100,000) ×
	Income ($100,000 - $125,000) ×
	Income (over $125,000) ×
	Choose income ┊ Browse
	More Demographics ▼
Interests	Search interests ┊ Suggestions ┊ Browse
Behaviors	**Residential profiles**
	Likely to move
	Search behaviors ┊ Browse

At this point, we have the ads set up. You'll want to set up the budget at something about $200- $500 per month. I would recommend you begin with $350 per month. The Facebook advertisements for real estate do create a scalable source leads for you. You can choose to turn them up or down and spend however much you want to on them.

You should also click the part labeled 'optimize for clicks' and 'manually set your Bid per click'. Fix the bid $.10 over the maximum recommended amount.

Now head back and repeat the entire process for two of your articles.

You now have your Facebook Ads to show your message to prospective homebuyers within the area. They will be directed to your website where you'll get their phone number, email address and name.

What to do each day when running the Facebook ads

Since your ad is set up; the next thing you have to do is monitor it only once per day. While you're monitoring them, ensure you adjust your cost per click up or down based on the recommendation of Facebook and how much impression you're able to see. If your ad is not being shown to anyone, it means you are too low with your bid- you will easily detect this when your number of impressions stop changing every day.

Second, you can monitor the images you use on your Facebook ads. These images have a great impact on conversion. Some of them will convert better than others. You can use those images and delete the rest.

Turn off the ads that seem to cost more per click than the rest and then go over to the ad that is cheapest and click 'create similar ad'. Change the image into something similar to that ad (but that which is still different).

This will assist you in finding the best converting ad. It might take you a month to find the best one.

Lastly, you can set up three headlines and monitor the one that converts the best and consider shutting one of them off.

To validate this ad spend, let's do some math:

The math for Real Estate Facebook Ads

Usually, 10 percent of the Facebook ads clicks will give you their email address or phone number or both. You should always aim to produce better articles and content in general on your site until you get higher than the 10 percent conversion rate.

I'm sure you have a number at the back of your mind that turn into finished transactions. You can use the formula below to justify the ad cots:

Monthly Ad Spend / Cost Per Click = Total Clicks To Website

Clicks * Conversion Rate = Total Number Of Leads

Leads * Your Close Rate = Total Houses Sold

Alternatively:

$350 (total amount you spend in a month) / $0.35 (the average cost per click = 1000 clicks to your website

The 1000 clicks * the 10% conversion rate = 100 contacts

100 leads * Y% (your conversion rate) = Y properties sold

These are simple equations that should assist you validate the $350 ad spend. Once you find a profitable funnel, you can now open up the budget and gage it.

Google AdWords

Google AdWords is the system developed by Google to help you market your services and products in Google Search Engine, including its affiliate sites through the use of a placed text advertisement which pops up when people are searching for phrases related to what you're offering- which appears as a 'sponsored link'. The system is basically a pay-per-click system, which means you can direct where your advertisement should appear via bidding for a sequence of phrases. You also pay the amount you have bid for only if somebody clicks on your ad.

The ad appears on the results page you want to appear in; for example, the first page of Google for a search result. Your ads will appear to the right side and top of the organic search results. Through the amount of money you bid, you can also pitch at the spot on the page you want your ad to appear. This may crudely mean the more you bid for a phrase, the higher your ad appears on the first page of the search results.

You have to note that most people rarely scan past the first page of the search results, and also that the higher your website is located on a page, the more visitors your website gets because web users generally prefer clicking on the search results or ads at the top of the page.

To set up Google AdWords, just follow steps at https://www.entrepreneur.com/article/237212.

Video Marketing: Use the Viral Video Strategy

Viral videos are not just sloppy or amateur videos of dogs doing funny things or celebrities doing weird things. In fact, some of the best viral videos have been produced professionally by companies to be able to reach their audience differently.

When it comes to real estate, a viral video is one that promotes a property creatively, including a real estate company or an agent (or both) by use of content that draws attention and inspires viewers to want to share it with other people.

What makes a video go viral?

Viral videos in what can often be a pretty conservative industry ought to have one or most of a number of the characteristics to be able to achieve the success of an average viral video, which include:

Funny-The easiest way to get your video to go viral quickly is by making it funny. Nonetheless, there is a catch: working out what funny is to your target audience. There is nothing as bad as a video that is trying to be funny but is either way off the mark or tasteless. Therefore, make sure you know your audience pretty well before creating any video you wish to go viral.

Creative- You know your video is creative when another person watches it and says 'ah, wish I'd thought of that.'

Creativity is respected in all social circles and can do a great job at attracting the interest of viewers.

Short- If you go over some of the best viral videos on YouTube, you'll realize that most of them are actually less than five minutes long. The viral videos spread very quickly largely because most of them are extremely easy to absorb and watch many times.

Memorable- You'll know your video has gone viral when folks begin referring to it by name and if people can remember your video, they are most probably going to contact you when they want to do business.

The process of making a video is quite simple and straightforward:

How to make a real estate marketing video

Log in to https://app.picovico.com/login

Gather the pictures and video clips you want to use. Assuming you want to make a video about a particular real estate property (a bungalow, maybe). All you require is taking as many attractive photos and video clips as possible and filtering the best ones to include in the video.

Select the style you want to use. You have to choose a style at the beginning of your video making process. For the real estate videos, I might suggest you go for styles such as Frameless and circle but you can use any other style you think would be suitable for the video.

Upload the media files. You can now upload all your clips and photos you want to use onto the workspace in the site. For the music, I would suggest you use the free or commercially useable music since you will be using the video for purposes of branding or advertising.

Preview and complete. Take a preview of the video to see how it will look like and then you decide whether to go back to editing or just finalize the video. After that, you'll be allowed to add a title to your video followed by a description.

Save and share. Once the video is complete, you can download it and upload it to any platform you want such as YouTube, Vimeo or even the Picovico video page.

https://youtu.be/IF6anKHo1lU a good example of what I'm talking about.

Write regular newsletters

Real estate newsletters can be an effective marketing tool for keeping your name top of mind with your current clients, past clients, your prospects as well as your sphere of influence. They deliver your message, reinforce your brand and demonstrate your expertise- which is what a successful marketer does regularly.

The steps of creating newsletters

I am going to use MailChimp to describe this process. MailChimp is one of the best services for email marketing campaigns today especially because it has great free packages.

Gather your news

You have to spend quite some time gathering great content if you are to have a great newsletter. If you are sending a monthly newsletter, save some articles you find during the month in a special folder so that you have the entire content in a single area. You can get your content from anywhere- for instance, when you meet your friends, workmates (during staff meetings), let them know that you are looking for articles and request them to share their wisdom.

You can also go through the internet to get great content ideas, which could be about the following:

- The current market statistics- this means numbering the homes that are listed for sales, giving the medium or average listing and the sale price, and also the average days on the market. Make sure to interpret the data you present, explain well what it means and show how it is trending over time.

- The properties sold recently- sellers and buyers love seeing what has sold recently. Make sure you follow your brokers and the rules and regulations in your local state on what and how to present the current sales.

- The upcoming activities- It is recommended that you have a list or calendar of forthcoming events and or activities in a given area. This is important because most real estate newsletters tend to be very much targeted for a given geographical location. It sort of helps keep the newsletter 'sticky' and gives folks a reason to keep your newsletter and refer back to it multiple times.

- A CTA (call to action) - Getting your name and message out is important and a newsletter should also contain a CTA to inspire engagement. You can give a free home valuation/CMA. Insert a link to a webpage that is specifically created for that particular newsletter to enable recipients to go and download any information that they might be looking for. Try doing a CTA that informs people how you can set them up for automatic updates for listing.

- The seasonal tips- you can also include a short article and perhaps links to articles on issues related to taxes. You need to keep it specific to real estate and if possible, add some info about mortgage deduction.

Is the school about to resume? Include back to school tips where people can find school supplies.

Other things you can include are:

- More financial news- such as rate cuts, home loans, first home owner grants and new laws.

- Home improvement news and tips

- Time specific news- such as home security tips and news during the holidays

- Process news – such as the selling and purchasing processes of homes

Edit the news

After gathering your content, scan your article for simple things like sentence construction and grammar mistakes. In any case, the best articles are typically ones that are short and sharp. Make sure the article heading matches the content and take out any industry jargon or waffle.

NOTE: If you've never worked with MailChimp before, you can read http://mailchimp.com/resources/guides/getting-started-with-mailchimp/ to get started in case you find yourself getting lost anywhere.

Create your list

This is basically the list of the email addresses of people you want to receive your newsletter. When you create an account and sign in to MailChimp, you can start by creating your mail out list.

4. Create your campaign. Click on good ol' regular campaign if this is the first time you are doing this.

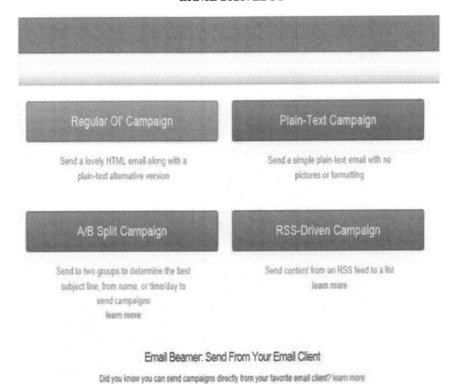

After creating the list, pick this list and begin entering the details about your campaign- or the newsletter.

The templates

Depending on how you want your newsletter to appear, you can pick any options from the ones below:

If you want to have full control over the layout and are good with code, you can write (code) your own.

If you still want to have control and are not confident that you have enough coding skills to take up the challenge, then perhaps the 'drag and drop' option is ideal for you.

However, if you want an option that has no fuss, you can select the pre-designed option. Let me demonstrate the predesigned option for you.

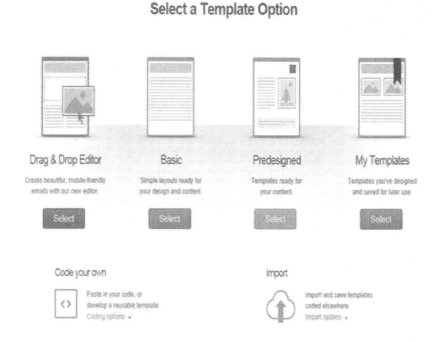

The good thing with MailChimp and services like it is that everything is done for you and anyone who has limited or exposure to the online newsletters will find it very simple. Just click on the templates on the column to the left and select a design that best fits your business.

Design

As you will notice, the options here are endless – we are thus going to cover a few of them that will be relevant and helpful to making your newsletter match your business branding. This is where you start to insert your content and change background and the font colors so that your newsletter remains unique to you.

Just click the boxes you would want to edit and begin to insert the news you collected. Simple!

The dashboard, which is similar to those in email programs that appear when you click in the box will contain all the tools you require to insert photos, change font size and color, use bullet points and so on.

Our real estate agency is the best in the area...

Confirm and preview the newsletter

When you're satisfied with the images and content, click confirm and go over what you've created using the preview button. If everything is okay, just follow the simple steps to finish the process.

Click send

Your newsletter will make your customers glad. If you used relevant and interesting content that shows your company is unique and a leader in the field to create your newsletter, your customers and prospective clients will remember you when they require your services.

Don't forget that in this program, the possibilities are endless so the next time you log in, be sure to check out what else you can do in the program and use it for your marketing program.

Offline Strategies

We have a number of offline marketing strategies you can employ to make prospective real estate buyers and sellers to contact you. Also, unlike the online strategies, most of them are really straightforward and less taxing.

For instance, we have

Bandit signs

Bandit signs are little variations of the usual billboard that are placed on walls or staked into the ground to act as the first point of contact for potential buyers (or sellers) and agents or marketers.

When drafting a design for your bandit signs, you have the option of visiting your local signs designer or look for a website that specializes in this field. When you're just starting out, make sure you order around 200 bandit signs while taking into account that a great number of them will be torn down or go missing.

Billboard signs

To take your marketing efforts up a notch, you could rent a billboard and the easiest way is through an advertising agency. The costs vary a lot depending on the location and the agency itself. For a billboard measuring 14' by 48', for instance, you can expect to part with the following cash for a four-week rental:

$3,000- Atlanta, Georgia

$1,200-Albuquerque, New Mexico

$3,100- Indianapolis, Indiana

The location of the billboard is very important so make sure the billboard is located in an area, which many people pass through so that the billboard is effective. You should also consider the number of people that drive by every day and how much the drivers can actually see the billboard.

For more information about renting a billboard, visit https://www.lendvo.com/guide-renting-billboard/.

Local media interviews

Getting a media interview can be difficult and that's why it's not the best idea to keep calling your local media house requesting for an interview. The best wat to get your name in front of the program directors and news directors is by writing and issuing relevant and pertinent press releases.

These need to be properly written and have to discuss critical issues of significance to their viewers. When you begin establishing yourself as an illustrious real estate expert, your phone will ring more often. These media appearances can really increase your exposure and advance your brand name recognition, which can bring about increased investment deals due to the perceived idea that you are an expert in the field. Many people that you'll be trying to sell properties to or those you will be trying to buy properties from will perhaps already know you. As such, they are likely to be more trusting thanks to your reputation within the local community.

Seminars

You can also give free seminars in a niche that is related to real estate to grow the size of your portfolio. As a residential real estate agent, you could consider giving a free seminar about topics as extensive as "The best ways to sell your property for a price in a down market" to "Buying a home with terrible credit." The important thing here is not to market yourself directly but come across more like a financial planner. Show your prospective customers what you know, and how you can help them; they will be glad to show their money later on.

Public speaking

Public speaking does not usually appear like a natural offline real estate marketing strategy, but it has potential that many people fail to consider. Most people are not natural public speakers; and do not quail if you are one of them. You can start by joining your local Toastmasters club and training with the best in the art of public speaking. Even as you are learning, you will be exposed to community and business leaders, many of whom have cash and (or) connections and could thus turn to be prime candidates to do business with.

Inform everyone you know and in your networks

Every so often, fresh investors make their first deals with family and friends, and more so, the referrals they can offer. All the exceptional real estate marketing ideas in the world cannot make up for a formidable social network that can easily point you toward your first acquisition.

Nonetheless, the deals that fall into your laps cannot really materialize until people know you are in the business. Therefore, even before you make the leap, just tell them, and prepare them to work with you as you begin. Word of mouth is simple but also a great tool, which some people argue is one of the top most in real estate marketing.

So, just begin telling people what you are about because you never know from where that elusive first deal might arise.

Other strategies you could also use include the following:

- Magazines: Real estate magazines are a goldmine for real estate deals so make sure to use them

- MLS (Multiple listing service)

- Telemarketing: This is where you cold-call prospective customers to spread your company's message. You could call them yourself or use a call center to make large volume sales. You could use the calls as an opportunity to call your current clients to get feedback about their satisfaction, talk about new listings, contact houses that are listed as sale by owner etc.

- Direct mail: Just mail potential clients directly; make sure to package your marketing material in a captivating manner to ensure it stands out from the many mails that the customer might receive. In the mail, don't let it to scream 'buy my product'; make sure you have something useful in your mail e.g. an open house, the ideal time to move etc.

- Referrals from current clients: You could offer to incentivize them in a way. You could send gifts/cards to your clients during special occasions e.g. Christmas, birthday, thanksgiving, anniversary, housewarming etc. then remember to mention your referral program

- Network: Don't just rely on your social networks for leads; you could participate in chambers of commerce and various networking groups to meet prospective customers. Make sure that you are an active member of any organization that you join, as this will ensure you stand out from everybody else. Being active means attending seminars and various other meetings, being very active in organizing other seminars, sponsoring an event etc. Another creative way is to build mutually beneficial relationships with some of the participants in those groups whereby the other person offers something, just as you do. If you are into commercial real estate, you may want to attend broker meetings to help you generate good leads that could ultimately bring in some sales.

- Brochures

- Flyers

- Radio ads

- Television ads

- Newspapers targeting the specific target market

I strongly believe that the above information will help you to make significant progress in generating qualified leads that could easily convert to paying customers. The question you might be having now is; how do you close the deals? Let's discuss that.

STEP 4: CONVERTING LEADS INTO CLOSED DEALS

By using the real estate marketing methods above, you will generate leads- but how do you convert these leads into real estate sales though?

Mainly, it's through follow-up and fulfillment.

Follow-up

According to statistics, about 48 percent of agents don't follow up with a prospect and 52 percent follow up at least once. Again, only 25 percent try contacting a prospect a second time and 12 percent try making three or more contacts.

You need to note that 80 percent of sales are made between the 5th to the 12th contact!

This essentially means that failing to retarget the lead is detrimental. When the lead mentions that they are not ready, you should not draw back but rather, keep contacting them and build a healthy relationship with the potential buyer; otherwise, he or she might get lost, feel ignored and perhaps fall into the hands of your competitor.

Therefore, you also need to get over the fear of offending your prospects by contacting them as many times as it takes because in real estate marketing, we say that by doing so, you are not badgering them, but being there when they are ready- because anyway, they are the ones who communicated that they are interested in the business.

Fulfillment

This simply refers to what you're giving them, the questions you are answering and the needs (of theirs) you are meeting.

Being there when they are ready is their most important need and it is accomplished through consistent follow-up. You also have to anticipate their questions and provide resources, answers and resolutions. While fulfillment is easier than follow-up it requires follow-up to accomplish. When you follow up, you meet their primary need.

Nurture the lead

The agents who begin their relationship by offering informative and efficient customer service have a greater chance to build a stronger psychological and social bond with a prospect.

This bond can easily override your competitors and even if they don't buy at first, they will most likely have a sense of loyalty that will drive them back to you.

Tip: Develop the habit of reading-through your contacts and updating them to a special excel sheet so that you are up to date with all of them. After that, make sure you categorize them as hot, warm or cold. The hot leads should be the ones that are ready to buy while the warm or cold leads are still weighing their options. You should therefore be with them through the decision process placing effort accordingly, as per the category they belong to.

At this point, I believe you are ready to implement your plan, and then evaluate later on. Before that though;

Do a quick analysis

Once you've known the basic elements of your real estate marketing strategy, you need to take a step back and review the details, making sure all you've planned is realistic.

Do you have considerable knowledge of your audience? Do you have the means to blog regularly (if you chose blogging as a strategy)? How about the timelines for success, are they practically possible? Comb over your plan before you begin to make sure you do not have to return to square one after months of work and reconfigure your marketing blueprint completely.

STEP 5: IMPLEMENT YOUR PLAN, EXAMINE YOUR TACTICS AND REPEAT

After setting your real estate marketing foundation, you can proceed to put everything into action. You can begin publishing landing pages, social media updates, blog posts, get your video and email strategies up and running or whatever else depending on what you selected as your marketing strategies, and begin implementing any other tactic you came across along the way you deem worthy of using.

After a period of about one month, take to Google Analytics and any other software you use to track and automate your marketing to go over the performance of your online marketing. Pin point what has worked so far, what has not and what you can do to advance your messaging, branding and eventually, bottom line.

In everything you do, realize that real estate marketing is like a machine that never stops- and this machine only grows stronger the more attention you pay to it and build upon it. You need to keep experimenting with fresh techniques you haven't tried yet and see whether they can assist you achieve your goals.

Commit yourself to specific tasks

From the little tasks such as getting a responsive website to the bigger tactics like developing an email campaign, you need to break down the kind of real estate marketing activities you are committed to doing over a specified period of time. You don't have to worry about taking on everything on all at once; but it is important to identify the lighter daily tasks you can perform in minutes and other tasks that need more time, effort and perhaps money (the long term tasks). Let's take a look at that in more detail.

The small short term tasks

Think of the important items you can take care of within short durations of time. For instance, you can include the following tactics to implement in your spare time:

- Brainstorm some blog post ideas everyday

- Segment your list of contacts for your email campaign

- Optimize you real estate marketing website for search

- Create a social media posting program or schedule

- Do a research of the options in market automation software

- Work little by little on a piece of long-form content such as an e-book

The basis of your plan of real estate marketing is built on executing these tasks, so you need to find time to work on them. Tasks like developing blog post ideas for real estate is a continuous process, since blogging never ends, you need to split your time evenly on things that you'll need to take care of regularly and one time tasks that require to be complete immediately.

The larger, long-term projects

On the other side, we have bigger marketing efforts, which you'll realize are usually activities related to lead generation, earning commissions and closing deals. In any case, the whole idea of marketing is to bring more sales- so you need to remember the large-scale goals that are sustained by your daily and weekly marketing activities.

After one month of blogging for example, you can examine your Google analytics to observe how your posts are doing. Ask yourself- how long do users spend on each page or post? How many sessions or views have I received?

Identify the metrics you'll build upon (in the online strategies)

Every real estate agent has one metric they would want to improve- their commission; when it comes to marketing though, you need to determine all the areas you'd want to improve. For instance, you want people to better know about your brand; thus, improving your web traffic could be a good goal to start with. If you're looking to ramp up lead generation, then having your site optimized with lead capture forms and capabilities should be your primary goal here. Perhaps you want to cultivate future sellers; this means that improving the email list could be your best bet. Just plan your real estate ideas around the metrics, whichever they are.

Perhaps (just like most beginners) you are not really sure about what could be the most important metrics for your marketing; you can check this graph from a report of content marketing institute and marketing profs. It shows what many professionals and brands out there consider the most essential metrics for their marketing. You have to note that getting site visitors is looked at as very crucial when it comes to success in online marketing- in any case, it's a substantial sales driver.

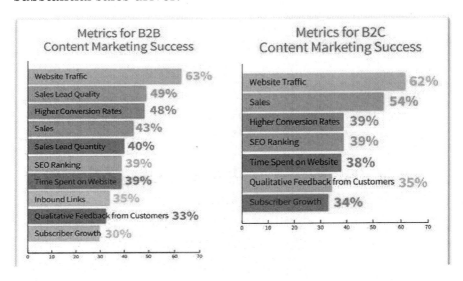

CONCLUSION

We have come to the end of the book. Thank you for reading and congratulations for reading until the end.

Many people usually have the dream of being successful with real estate marketing, but few of them know how to go about it. They don't know where to start, what to start with and how.

In this regard, the book has given you a plan that you can follow.

Use it as a blueprint- add whichever strategies you want to the ones already discussed and implement them when you're ready. Don't forget to do a proper analysis of the plan before implementation though and when you're done, evaluate everything, making sure to focus on areas that you could improve.

If you found the book valuable, can you recommend it to others? One way to do that is to post a review on Amazon.

Thank you and good luck!

Get Your Free Copy of

How to be a Real
Estate Millionaire

To Get Your Free Copy, Open the Link

https://ebraveboy_3ee2.gr8.com/